S0-ARP-079

Adeline Juneby Potts

Walk by the Spirit

By
Adeline Juneby Potts

Including
Our Last and Best Season
on the Trapline
By
Mike Potts

Jelm Mountain Press
1993

Walk by the Spirit

By Adeline Juneby Potts,
with "Our Last and Best Season On The Trapline"
by Mike Potts.

Copyright 1993 by Adeline Juneby Potts.

Cover by R. G. Finney, © 1993.

Scripture taken from the New American Standard Bible,
© 1960, 1962, 1963, 1968, 1972, 1973, 1975, 1977 by
the Lockman Foundation. Used by permission.

Jelm Mountain Press
Laramie, Wyoming
ISBN 0-936204-81-8

Dedication

For my Lord and Savior, and to my husband, Mike, who stood by me and taught me how to love again.

In the memory of my beloved parents Willie and Louise Juneby, my brothers, Charlie, Li'l Johnny, Archie and baby John and my sisters, Mary Ann, Sara and Margaret Carol. And in memory of our traditional Chief, Andrew Isaac and his wife Maggie.

Acknowledgments

Special thanks to my sister in Christ, Judy Lorenz and my new friend, Traci Zimmerman, for the many hours of typing, revising and editing. And to my brothers Isaac and Ben, along with my sister Ellen, my nieces and nephews, Aunty Caroline, Uncle Agnor, brothers-in-law, Silas, Mel and Dave. My sisters-in-law, Sandi and Cindy for their encouragement, cooperation and help along my trail of recall.

My nephew, Wild Bill, my parents-in-law, Sue and Bud and my two children, Sonny and Jody Ann, along with my little nephew, David, have all stood by me in their patience and taught me my patience.

Last, but not the least, I appreciate my dear friends, Sarah James, R. G. and Lynn Finney.

Some names have been changed to protect the privacy of those in the book.

Foreword

Adeline has worked long and hard getting into print the story of her family's triumph over many challenges of poverty, alcoholism, prejudice, disease and despair.

Adeline started in the summer of 1991, with spiral notebooks and a busy pen. Her family and several friends kept encouraging her to expand on victories, pleasant and painful memories. Adeline and her daughter Jody, traveled between Alaska and Wyoming, researched a prestigious family and tribal history, delved into languages and customs, and have set themselves even more goals. Her husband Mike, older son, Sonny, and nephew David along with numerous other family members have contributed time and ideas to see this dream become a reality.

You see, her first concern, when coming to me asking how to begin, was to be able to share her joy about whom she is and her pattern of triumph to others in need of a similar victory. Adeline and her family have deep compassion for Native Americans and others looking for peace, relief, and an assurance that there truly is a reason to live.

The most sensible way to get through difficult territory is to follow someone who knows the way or to use their maps. This family has accumulated their "life maps" into these pages for the benefit and encouragement of all readers.

The evidence of the Potts' family's victory is a "map" for you, the reader; follow it toward the knowledge of your value and your ability to have your own triumph.

Enjoy this story of joy, contentment, and love above suffering and misery. May God's great love and special blessings be showered upon you in the days to come.

Judy Ann Lorenz
Encampment, Wyoming
1993

Contents

I

II

Introduction

To the best of our knowledge, there is little known of the Han band of the Athabascan Indians or of their journey to the banks of the Yukon River (around the Alaska - Yukon Territory) where they came from or who was of any kinship to them elsewhere.

However at the Tower of Babel where God dispersed men to the ends of the earth, we can be sure that's where the journey began, some wheres about four thousand years ago it started. It's interesting to note, that many Indian tribes, including my own, believe that a world-wide flood occured and how only a single family survived to start mankind, but Sin has continually destroyed and caused much suffering to man, and its only through God's grace that we are able to endure and through God's mercy, He saves a remnant of all nations through the shed blood of His only Son Jesus Christ.

The Han Indian was no different than the Celts of Ireland, the further they got away from the Tower of Babel, the further they got away from God. As always, traditionally, man has turned away from God and (gone his own way) followed man.

The Han Indians were somewhat taller than the other Indians along the Yukon and the language is a little different.

Before alcohol started destroying them around the turn of the century, the first white trailblazers respected them very highly. According to Osgood's *The Han Indians*, they were also most feared. Now with alcohol there isn't much left of the Han Indians, there are fewer than one hundred that can speak the language and the once strong family institution is next to non-existant.

Our hope is that some of the Native Americans will see their sin, fear God, and see that Christ shed blood and death was the only payment for our sin that would satisfy God. Hence His death for our sins and resurrection is the only way to eternal peace.

Of all the changes and culture shock in my lifetime, as I have come from the trapline, mining camps and Indian village, gone from boarding school to college, if I were to re-live one stage of my life, I would choose to remain as I am today, A BORN AGAIN CHRISTIAN.

The pages that follow are the true life story of an Alaskan Indian; to the beginning of my memories as I lived and saw life.

Throughout my story you may shed some tears of sadness or of happiness. I have come to believe there is a reason for everything. For me to go back in memory, with many hours of writing and a few teardrops, has been a cleansing process which I did not anticipate. My goal at the beginning remains my goal now; to reach out to my people, the Native Americans. To assure them of God's love and the value of each and every one in the eyes of Almighty God.

With my life turning around, I am living for the Lord daily until He comes again as He promised. I pray that as a new believer in Christ with the help of the Holy Spirit, may you

WALK BY THE SPIRIT.

Walk By The Spirit
Galatians 5:16

I

1

Mining Camp and Trapline

A little, 14' x 16' cabin was "Home Sweet Home." Candles, kerosene lamps or in finer times, a Coleman gas lamp, gracing homemade tables surrounded by gasoline box chairs, were all that was needed for a cozy, candlelight feast on moose or caribou. No TV, telephone or such were available to us, but we were one big, happy family. We had each other and we were doing everything together. Sitting on the cool cabin floor, we played with our homemade dolls while Mom hummed along with the radio as she prepared our meals and Dad played cards at the kitchen table.

Today, as I sat in our 74'x14', three bedroom mobile home in Encampment, Wyoming, doing the bead work patterns of my people, I could visualize and remember most of my childhood days growing up on the winter trapline, spending summers in a mining camp in Woodchopper and Coal Creek, Alaska in the 40's.

My mother, Louise Mary Silas, was born and raised in Moosehide, Yukon Territory Canada. She stood a sturdy, round five foot, two inches. In her Athabascan Indian family, she was taught the Indian way of life. To be able to live off the land and to tan and sew hides were of great importance. Mother shared her skills with us during those early trapline and mining camp days.

My father, William Jim Juneby, also known as Willie, was born and raised in Eagle, Alaska. Part of his younger days were spent in Ketchumstock, out of Tok, Alaska. I have been told by a village elder in Eagle that his family may be from Whitehorse, Yukon Territory, Canada on the Yukon River. I am hoping someone may come forward to tell me more about the name "Juneby." Both my parents were of the Han band from the area between Dawson, Yukon Territory, Canada and Eagle Alaska.

Dad was a big man, over 6 feet tall; a good trapper, self-taught "cat skinner" (*Caterpillar* tractor operator) and a skilled fiddler.

Two kids are plenty for my husband, Mike, and me, but my parents enjoyed our big family and were well able to handle us. In later years, they even helped raise some of their grandchildren.

We grew up using only Athabascan Indian language in our family, but I recall whites working in the mining camps along with my father and other Indians. I believe these white, English speaking neighbors of our early childhood were our source for beginning to use English, which soon became our second language.

Mary Ann, Charlie and Isaac were born in Eagle and spent some of their early childhood there before my parents moved to the mining camps. They would have been more familiar with white people. But, for Sara, Li'l Johnny and me, the white men working in the mining camp were our first contact with these *Non-Dlees* (whites). We were timid at first, not knowing what to say to these tall, white guys. We would communicate through Mom and Dad. They taught us to be respectful, but being energetic, normal kids, once we got to know the guys, we did things like jump on their beds and general tearing around their lodgings. When it was time at last to go home and our tummies were full of candy, we would head for the footbridge over Woodchopper creek. We would be daring one another to run across without falling in. If Mom had ever known we did these things, she would never have allowed us to to visit the

2

Non-Dlees again! Strict was her middle name!

The mining camp in Woodchopper was surrounded by beautiful hills, wild flowers, and creeks, with a big, busy dredge at the end of the camp. There was an abundance of berries, game, and graylings. This was paradise! Coal Creek was about 100 miles from Eagle on the Yukon River. Here, too, was a picture of true, natural beauty. During the summers, fresh king salmon was caught from the Yukon.

In the middle of the Woodchopper mining camp was a sparkling, spotless mess hall, next to the runway and post office. The cook was a beautiful red-head named Flo. On the way back from the post office, Mom used to stop by the mess hall to say "Hi" and chat about things going on in the camp. We were shy, but intrigued by Flo's unusual and lovely red-hair. We would peek our heads through the doorway; our timid smiles would always be rewarded with baked bacon rinds, cookies or leftovers.

There were many in camp whom I can barely remember, but a few stand out in my memories. One special person was Phil Barail. A bachelor, his burly, rough and tough exterior covered a soft heart, and he put up with a lot from us kids. With his pants shiny from dirt and grease and his beard dripping with bear fat, even the grizzlies wouldn't come near him.

Like Dad, Phil worked in the mining camp and ran a trapline. He was camp postmaster as well. He built several cabins in the area he trapped. His main cabin was on the Yukon across from the Coal Creek camp. Mom and Dad enjoyed visiting with Phil, so sometimes after Dad got off work, we would all paddle across the river, or in winter, mush our dogteam across. The grownups would sit for hours and tell stories. I always liked going to Phil's house for despite our mischief, we would count on treats of candy and dried fruit. Later on the way home, "crunch, crunch," was the sound of the sled runners against the snow. Most of the time, I would be asleep for the homeward trip.

Harry Miller was a name and a man of mystery to everyone in the camp. Whether he was working or just

3

passing through, I do not know; he may have worked cleaning up the dredge. One day he vanished. Rumors flew like ducks flying south in the fall. "He may have been a spy," commented one miner. "He sure was a strange man, no one here could find out where he came from or if Harry Miller was his true name," said another. As a little girl, I had no fear of strangers, there was no need for fear in those days. And, we used to run up to Miller as we would any of the others. But a few times we became hesitant and backed off; children sensing a problem, if no threat to us.

Another favorite trapper and miner was Al Ames. Al was married to an Indian woman from Fort Yukon names Nina. They had five children about the same age as my oldest brothers, Charlie and Isaac. One of their daughters, Molly, lives in Fairbanks and a son, Albert, Jr. is in South Dakota. I do not know what has happened to the rest of the family. Al and Nina passed on some time ago.

In his book, *Coming into the Country*, John McPhee tells of Al Ames in 1943 and the survival of the B-52 that crashed in the area.

Those other hardworking men who are shadows in my memory were generous and patient. We would visit them, enjoy treats of candy and often overstay our welcome. Most of them did not have their families at the camp for the job was seasonal. From April to October they lived in bunkhouses and ate at the mess hall. I suspect we were certified nuisances, but these hardworking, family men sure enjoyed having our company! The days were peaceful and good; children weren't under threat of being snatched or molested. But times have changed and so have our lifestyles. Alcohol, drugs, abortion and greed were not the Indian way of life, only burdens we have acquired as we have tried to enter a fast-paced society.

One of the first changes I recall during our childhood was a happy one. My oldest sister, Mary Ann married Silas Stevens from Eagle Village. We impatient, younger ones often puzzled about her visits to Eagle till

4

we learned SILAS was the answer to our questions! Silas was just out of the Army when he met Mary Ann. They were such a handsome couple. They made their first home together in Nenana, Alaska. We missed Mary Ann, but we were proud of her and happy for her. Teenagers Charlie and Isaac began attending Indian boarding school in Wrangell and were only home during the summer.

Sara, Johnny and I were home and our family added Archie in 1950. Part of every day saw us all running and skipping towards the tailing piles where we waited for Dad on his way home. At first glimpse, we would race to him. Whoever got there first won the leftovers in his black lunch pail. He usually left an orange or cookies in the pail for this reason. Poor Li'l Johnny was nearly always the loser, so we ended up sharing with him.

Dad would run the "Cat" (*Caterpillar* tractor) all day long and when we climbed all over him, he would smell of diesel. To this day I still love the smell of diesel and prefer it over any shaving lotion.

One memorable 4th of July, the boys, just home from school, brought firecrackers. We were fascinated by this new entertainment. I had never seen a firecracker before. Dad showed off by lighting them for us. One blew up in his hand and so did Mom! She chewed him out good!

Mining camp life was comfortable and good to us. We had the privilege of getting fresh fruit, vegetables and eggs when we lived there. We lived in a lumber house, roomy and easier to keep than the log cabins. Mom would order most of our clothes from Sears and Roebuck. She used her artistic skills to make dolls for us out of the rags from the dredge. These rags were brought in to be used by the workers on the dredge to wipe up the oil. Mom would first make a pattern, then cut it out of the rag material, sew it together by hand, stuff it and embroider eyes, nose and mouth, topping our "baby" off with colored yarn hair.

Both mining camps were owned by Dr. Ernest Patty, who was the President of the University of Alaska in

Fairbanks. *Hah-Khee* was a name the Indians gave him; meaning in our language "Boss" or the "Big Shot." He was a husky man, as I recall, with a kind face. He and his wife and family flew in and out of camp. Once, I heard Mom describing Mrs. Patty as "a very lovely woman." The Indian families respected him because he respected them and gave them jobs. Whenever Ernie was around, we kids would always try to be on our best behavior and not act like a bunch of *siwash* (French word for people living in the woods).

Our closest neighbors were Doug and Lois Johnson. He was short and stocky, a happy go-lucky type of guy with a dogteam as fast as George Atta's team in Fairbanks. (George is an Alaskan Indian famous for winning the North American Championship races over ten times. In the 80's a movie was made in behalf of this great dog musher called *Spirit of the Wind.*) During the winter, while our family was on the trapline, Doug used to mush his dogs over the hills braving the cold, to bring news, groceries and *Hershey* bars to our cabin. Lois and Doug had five children, Marian, Esther, Bertlyn, John, and Rachael. Lois, like Mom, was busy taking care of the kids. There were no working Mom's in those days; they already had a full-time job.

Larry and Betsy Davis and their three children, Shawna, Dwayne and Larry, Jr. were another family who were special during our growing-up years on the trapline and in the mining camps. Later, they moved to Eagle and added five more children to their family. If there was a definition for being kind, it was Betsy. Larry was a hard worker and a good provider. In the fall when the blueberries were ripe, Larry would come by our house with Hills Brothers coffee cans in both hands.

"By gosh, Willie, I'm going to pick berries." he would tell Dad, spitting snuff from the side of his mouth as he spoke. In our custom, picking berries, gathering wood or taking care of freshly killed moose or caribou was *trin jah wew ptré* (woman's work). I like the saying, "A woman's job is never done." Dad would answer, "Larry, you worked all day, you must be tired." Whether he

6

heard Dad or just ignored him, Larry would head off into the woods with his wirehandled coffee can 'buckets'.

The three families were like one big, happy family, always finding something productive to do, picking berries, stringing beads, sledding or doing chores, it was all fun and a part of our daily life. Of course, we had our spats, one time I threw some pepper in a couple of the girls' faces! Or eating Jell-o which Betsy had put in the cold creek water to jell for dinner. When my parents found out, we had to make our own dessert to replace the Jell-o and pay the consequences by doing chores.

Of all our chores, I hated packing water. There was a weasel by the creek that I was petrified of. Getting water was one of the chores which was part of our punishment for the Jell-o incident.

I have to say that Sara, being older, usually was the better schemer, with Li'l Johnny and I being her followers. Once she had a plot to play a trick on old Phil Barail by scaring him half to death the next time we went for a visit. I don't recall all the details which were probably more exciting in kids' imaginations than in real life. But, Mom and Dad were with us on our next visit and the scary trick never came about.

Mom often told us stories to occupy us in the evenings. They were ones she made up, but were like most fairy tales. Most nights she would start with tales of Jack Frost, a snowy-looking creature who went from house to house in the middle of winter to check if all good kids were in bed. Whenever the temperature dropped to 50 degrees below zero, the frozen ground would crack with a big bang. "That's Jack Frost checking up," said Mom. It didn't take long before we were sound asleep. Another story character I vividly remember was a bird named Bii-Soo which we identified as a woodpecker living near our cabin. He was wiser than an old owl, sitting on a tree watching every move. We never heard of Goldilocks or Bambi until years later. There were no books; but I do recall *Life* magazine and *Alaska Sportsman* laying around the house. My family practiced the Indian tradition of communication; telling lots and lots of stories.

Mom made our winter gear—mukluks out of Indian tanned moosehide and our hats out of martin hides and tanned beaver hides became our mittens. She also made the sewing sinew, using tendons found along the back of moose or caribou and made into strong thread to hold leather stitching. Mom and her neighbors were very knowledgeable in case of emergencies and with no pharmacy just down the street. For infection from cuts, they would use spruce pitch (sap from the spruce tree) to draw the infection from the wound. Boiled tea bags were used on infected eyes. Some wild plants relieved certain rashes, others helped other problems. Camomile flowers were one herb she used.

Our trapline cabin sat amongst a bunch of spruce trees. Next to it was the *cache* (French for hiding place). We stored our food in the cache to protect it from varmints. Similar to a miniature cabin sitting atop poles at each corner, the cache was sometimes over 6 feet from the ground. On one side of the cabin was a big hill covered with birch, and spruce trees. I remember the sight as being one of the most beautiful I ever expected to see, as we sledded under a full moon, with snowshoe rabbits running every which way. Mom would yell, "Time to come in" on her way to the outhouse. I complained and made a fuss about coming in too soon, so Sara decided to come out earlier the next time. Only, we didn't know how to tell time; during the winter it got dark early, by 2:30 pm and by the time we got up in the mornings, it was dark until nearly 8:30 am. These times were the happiest in my life.

Whenever Dad would go and check the trapline or on a hunt for meat, we would all wait up for him on the night Mom expected him home. She would hear him talking to the dogs long before we could see them. "Gee, Haw, or Whoa." Dad would yell, as well as rewarding praises, "Good Dogs," or "Time to Eat." *Gee* meant turn right, *Haw* was turn left. They seemed to understand every word he said. Happy to be home, they would wag their tails, jumping all over him as he unharnessed and chained them up, one by one. He fed them warm fish

8

scraps mixed with oatmeal or rice.

As soon as he stepped through the door, Mom would check to see if he had any blood on his clothing. Blood was a sign he had killed a moose or caribou. She NEVER went outside to check the toboggan (a type of sled pulled by the dog team). She knew he was a good hunter and hardly ever feared for him when he was gone. The next day we would have a big feast; kidneys which tasted like chicken gizzards and heart like that of a cow. For the next several days, Mom would cook moose head soup, or roasted caribou head, or tongue soup with piles of Indian fried bread covered in butter. There is nothing tastier than this. Mom bought butter in a can; most of our food was either canned or dried.

Most of the time, Dad would return from the trapline with his toboggan full of marten, fox, wolves or wolverine. He was a successful hunter and trapper. As long as he had his dog team, he had it made!

Indian people all across the country never wasted any part of the animals. They believe that God the creator gave the animals to us for our use. We used every bit from the hides to the legs to the heads. I cringe at the sight of meat being wasted, expecially the best parts like the moose or caribou heads. Not long ago, I read an article about poachers in the *ALASKA* magazine; there in the middle of the tundra was a caribou carcass minus the trophy head. I'd love to track the poacher or poachers down, make them feed the hungry for the rest of their lives and display the trophy in an old outhouse.

During the cold spell, one December, Dad told Mom that he was mushing to Woodchopper to pick up the mail and all our Christmas packages from Sears. I think this was a two day trip, so Mom made sure he had enough food and dry clothing in case he ran into an overflow from one of the creeks along the way and got wet.

Dad's sleddogs were half wolf. We were never allowed to go near them by ourselves, for they had a wild instinct about them. I've heard Dad tell the story of taking Charlie with him to check the trapline when Charlie was a little boy. Dad only turned his back a minute when the

9

dogs turned on Charlie, getting tangled in their harness. I imagine this tangle kept them from having time to get at him before Dad yelled. As big as he was, those dogs obeyed him fast! One dog was a pet and may have been one of the leaders. We named him Jickle and he was the only one allowed in the house, more for protection and for us to play with. We would hitch Jickle to our homemade mini sled and the three of us would take turns riding. Sometimes the turn taking led to quarreling among ourselves and Mom would step in with a dire warning of "No dessert tonight." Most of the time dessert was boiled prunes with whipping on top. Mom would set a can of evaporated milk outside to chill, add a little sugar then she whipped it up with an egg beater. On special days, she made pies of dried fruits or jello.

On the night Dad went to Woodchopper, Mom was left alone with the three of us. After getting us to bed, she usually sat at the table sewing beads, listening to the radio, or reading her Bible. All of a sudden she was spooked by a movement outside the window. Like an angry old sow bear looking after her cubs, her first concern was for us. She turned the radio and the lights down; then she realized it was a reflection from the moon and some clothes flapping back and forth on the clothes line. Just imagine being out in the middle of nowhere; you begin thinking all kinds of things. By now I was used to falling asleep with the radio on and woke up to the same station playing country and western music.

This brings me back to the time when another Indian family had settled down for the night. As they slept, a grizzly bear broke through one of the cabin windows. The noise woke them in time for the wife to ward him off with a chair which kept him from climbing through the window. The children were all huddled in terror in one corner on the bed while their father was trying to get past the window to reach for his gun on the porch/walk-in entry of the cabin. Finally, after what seemed like forever, he got his gun. He fired one shot and wounded the bear, but it got up and walked away.

10

This was very unusual for a wounded bear to do, but thankfully, this one did. This incident happened in Woodchopper while my family was at Coal Creek. My friend in Eagle still remembers this as does the brave woman who fought a grizzly bear with a chair. Thinking of it scares me to this day.

What happened that night at our neighbors' house was beyond our belief, but it was God's protection. For later in life, this mother became a strong Christian woman who always gave. You never went away from her house hungry. She and my dad were neighbors in Eagle in later years. They served gallons of tea to strangers passing through Eagle. My kids, Sonny and Jody Ann, called this Spirit-filled woman the *"Goodies Grandma."*

Indians never eat bear meat, especially grizzlies, considering the animals to be bad spirits. The Indians believed the bears knew and understood when the people talked to them. The women never allowed a baby to cry when out in the woods picking berries, fearing the bears would mistake the baby for a cub. They claim a baby's cries are very similar to the cries of a cub when heard at a distance. John McPhee worded my fears well in his book *Coming into the Country.* "There might be taste, but there was terror in the bear." John jotted as he sat in our little cabin in Eagle, eating grizzly steaks with my husband Mike one night after they had checked the fish nets. Mike replied, "This is a fat starved country," while inhaling the steak and fat.

Another time during the summer, Charlie, Isaac, Sara and I were playing outside. Mom came out to call us and saw a grizzly bear coming towards us for free dinner. She never used a gun; there wouldn't have been time. Instead, she ran up to the bear and said in Indian, "Leave us alone and have mercy on us." The bear turned and wandered off. This may have been a one time incident, but it followed the belief of the Indian women that if you speak to a bear in the Indian language, it will sense and understand.

SUMMER—1951. The time and season stand in my mind as the beginning of tragedy and loss in my life. All

I had known was the closeness and love of these three families and being very young, I expected our life to continue so forever.

On a hot, quiet day, at Snare Creek, near Coal Creek, Mom had to take Archie, suffering with pneumonia, to the hospital via the mail plane. She left very early before Dad went to work. He got himself around and off to work, and we children were supposed to get ourselves up and go to the neighbors for the day. Suddenly there was a lot of commotion going on. I asked, "What's going on?" Our friends, Betsy and Lois were running to our house, yelling at us to get out. No one ever had time to answer my question. My next memory is of sitting on the hill and watching our house burn to the ground. A radio Lois retrieved by reaching through a window was the only thing left of our belongings.

Some of my favorite memories are of a loving and friendly family gathered around the table for my father's storytelling, these tales are some sad, some happy, some funny, and all true. One of my parents' favorite stories was about the plane trip to Fairbanks.

In March of 1947, when I was only 11 months old, Mom, Dad and I were flying to Fairbanks via the Eagle summit, near Circle. Mom was pretty close to giving birth to my brother Johnny. Flying over the summit with turbulance all around, the plane hit the side of a hill and crashed. It was a miracle we survived. When relating this story, Dad used to declare, "There was NO contact with the airport; the aerial was so messed up."

Between the pilot and Dad, they got the aerial fixed and made radio contact. A rescue plane soon flew over and dropped some survival gear. We used the wrecked plane for shelter and made the best of the situation in order to survive.

Dad would continue the story, "There was no time for panic, just use your head. But, Mom wasn't feeling too well." There was a small sled, wherever it came from I don't know, probably from the rescue plane. They used it to pull Mom over the hill, then Dad came back to get me. They had set me up on top of the hill knowing as

12

long as they could see me and I could see them, I would be okay.

With a smile on his face, but at the same time licking his lips when recalling the stress, Dad kept telling us the story. "We were airlifted. All our troubles are behind now . . . until Mom went into labor." With me as a co-pilot, Dad helped deliver Willie Juneby, Jr. in the back seat. The new pilot had turned around just a few minutes before and asked her if she could wait twenty minutes. "It's only twenty minutes more," they could remember him saying. There was no waiting for Li'l Johnny as he came into this world on a cold March day. He may have gotten the name Johnny from the pilot who flew us to Fairbanks. If that man is alive today, he would be in his late 60's or his 70's. Some of the elders in Eagle might recall this pilot's name. Later, the *Alaska Sportsman* had an article about the incident which could be found at the Fairbanks Library.

"Time for baths," mom would tell us as she tried to do two things at a time. How I dreaded the baths; this meant I had to go and face that old weasel down by the creek. I made sure that there were others heading down at the same time before I got my bucket of water. This was the summer that my Uncle from Eagle got a job at the mining camp. He and his wife and son lived up the street from us in a frame house the camp provided. Mom was out of face soap and it was bath time. "Adeline, run up to your Uncle's and borrow a bar of Ivory soap." I was still learning English. How do you say soap in Indian, let alone in English? Once up there, I was truly lost for words, especially "soap." I used "*Kut-Kut*" in the place of "soap." No one knew what I was talking about; it sounded like a foreign language I had invented! That is the story of how I got my Indian name, "***Kut-Kut***."

After Li'l Johnny, there was a baby girl born in 1948 and named Margaret Carol. She was delivered by a mid-wife. I once was told she was born in Ft. Yukon. She died as an infant from meningitis. She didn't live long enough to have a chance in life. Mom told stories about her as if she had been with us forever. She always had

Mom and Dad, March 1947, a few days
after Li'l Johnny was born on the airplane

tears in her eyes, but I was too young to understand a
mother's loss in the death of a child.

"What's going on?" Dad yelled in the middle of the
night. The next thing I knew he had the spot-light on
us— he kept a flashlight on his homemade bed stand.

The ruckus was in answer to an old problem. Li'l Johnny was afraid of the dark and many nights he woke up, got scared and climbed into bed with Sara and me, much to our irritation. Well, on this particular night, Sara had been beating on me, thinking it was Li'l Johnny. My loud, if sleepy protest had awakened Dad. Half asleep and not knowing what was going on, I soon went back to sound sleep as if nothing had happened. And the rest of the family settled down for the remainder of the night too. These years were the best parts of our lives. I had no idea other places existed, like Eagle and Fairbanks or Encampment,Wyoming. Even when the Alaska towns were mentioned, they seemed unreal to me. We thrived in our own little world. No electric bill, or insurance on cars, houses or medicine. Or having to get up in the middle of the night to the phone's ringing, wondering who's calling with some bad news, only to have it be a wrong number.

We never knew words like "stress," "child abuse," etc. . . . Our lives centered around the joys of winter and the joys of summer!

Going back to our summers in camp, Charlie and Isaac used to come home from the boarding school all grown up. Suddenly there was something different about these guys! They knew how to READ! They took us fishing for graylings in the tailing piles and read to us. How we loved those times. All fishing trips were important to us. There were times when we would get into fights, finally Mom or Dad would step in and threaten us with our fishing privileges to bring peace.

My next most significant memories are of Mary Ann's family. We were all so excited when she gave birth to her son, Walter Silas Stevens. Mom and Dad were so proud. We were one happy household when they heard about their first grandchild over the radio station KFAR out of Fairbanks. Sara, Li'l Johnny and I woke to my parents' glowing faces as Dad cooked pancakes with blueberries. While cutting into the big slab of bacon, he and Mom just about did the jig! All of Alaska knew on that cold January day about Juneby's new grandbaby!

Mary Ann was short and pretty with two big dimples on each cheek. She and Silas started such a lovely family and today I treasure each one of my beloved sister's children. Next came Regina Marie, known as 'Regi' today, followed by Sophie Clara, William Arthur 'Billy', and Deborah Louise 'Debbie'. Sophie was given the nickname *"Soot-Toot"* by both grandpa's; she was the apple of her grandpa's eyes.

Sophie lives in Fairbanks these days and is the co-ordinator for the FAS program. FAS—Fetal Alcohol Syndrome—a cause of mental retardation and numerous birth defects caused by the mother's intake of alcohol during pregnancy. Across our nation, Indian people are the hardest hit with over 5,000 babies born victims of FAS each year. I have been told Alaska was leading #1 in Satan's latest scheme on our people. I often wondered if the mothers would continue to drink if they knew *they* would suffer some harm like being disabled for the rest of their lives. But, they continue to drink, because of their selfish desires and bring an innocent child into the world who will be the one to pay for the mother's folly. Michael Dorris, a Native American, tells about FAS in his book, *The Broken Cord*. We talk about protecting people's rights. What about the rights of the unborn? Abortion is another sin that is acceptable in this society. Killing babies seems to be the easy way out. In Psalm 139: 13-16 of the Holy Bible it talks about the Lord's formation of man. Some believe babies go to heaven when they die. I sure hope it's right.

Debbie inherited her good looks from her Mom. Regi and Sophie got what most of us women today would envy; their Mom's good figure and dimples. Billy is married to Ula and lives in Fairbanks. He's tall like Grandpa Willie and likes to live a quiet life. His mother nicknamed him "Sam Bolo." Walter is another tall, handsome man; got his smiling eyes from Silas. Silas's parents were Arthur and Sophie Stevens of Eagle Village. These children were the pride and joys of both sides of the family.

16

2

Move to Eagle

When we moved to Eagle in the 1950's to go to school, a local store owner from Eagle and his son (who later became my brother-in-law) came to Coal Creek in a massive boat to pick up the other two families. The night they were to leave, Mom and Dad decided to send Sara and I along. Laying in bed at the "Slaven" cabin, it was scarey just thinking of going into another world. We'd heard stories of Eagle and some of the family we'd never met. The trip to Eagle took all day for this boat load of people (packed in like sardines), with one stop for lunch and several pit stops. In the darkness, we could see distant lights; flash lights on the bank of the Yukon. Whoever they were, they knew exactly when the "Boat People" were arriving. We were unloaded and hauled in a pick-up truck and a van to the village. I asked Sara in Indian, "Where are they taking us?", at the same time hanging on to her and hoping they wouldn't separate us. Once we were in the village, we were introduced to Mary Ann's in-laws, Sophie and Arthur. Sophie was a motherly type, wearing an apron. A nice looking woman with salt and pepper hair which she kept from around her face with a scarf fixed like a bonnet. I noticed right off she was always spitting something out every so often into an old coffee can. We found out later it was snuff. I recognized Arthur as a smart man because he spoke both English and Indian well. He was short and dark with a stern look. He was the Chief of the village, but what was a Chief? I didn't understand and it didn't matter. I

17

wanted to go back to Coal Creek to Mom and Dad or go to where the other two families were. But we were told there was no room for us at their cabins. Arthur was a kind and gentle person; he tried to please us by offering everything from candy to dried fish. That night I cried myself to sleep.

I woke up to hear someone moving around the house. It was warm and the Coleman lamp was burning. I nudged Sara and tried to wake her so I wouldn't have to face these two strangers by myself. Next thing I knew, they were cooking rice and raisins and biscuits for us. Pretending to be asleep,I heard every word they said. They spoke in Indian and mostly about the every day affairs of the village, which didn't make any more sense to me than the business about a Chief. Sara helped me get dressed and washed my face and combed my hair. She was only two years older, but today she was my Mom.

Next door to Sophie and Arthur were Dorothy and Jim Juneby. Dorothy was very nice and told us that we were related to them because Jim was Dad's nephew and our cousin. They had two children at the time; the girl was just a baby. We were quiet and standing by the door. I hung onto Sara. As quick as we could we ran out the door without saying a word. We walked down the street. Soon a couple boys came towards us pulling a coaster sled; the kind from Sears & Roebuck. Sara made a comment about the sled. The children stared at us, but went on by without saying a word. Then we turned back up the village street toward the house where we had spent the night. Just past that house we found the family we had come up with in the boat. We had *found our family!*

Two days later, Mom arrived in a Norsman plane with Li'l Johnny and Archie and Dad's dogs. The airline was operated by Wiens Airlines. One of their bush pilots was Don Holchizer. Don used to stop in Woodchopper on his way to Eagle and back to Fairbanks, we knew who he was. He and his wife spent their summers in Eagle. Since we knew Don, very soon we were going into town to visit and play at their house. The cabin they lived in

Sunday School Class in Eagle. L to R - Front row; Sara, Ethel, Adeline (me), George, Tony, Bertha, Li'l Johnny and Micah. Back row, L to R.;Mary Ann, Angela, Mary, Tim and Fred.

remains on main street today. Their daughter became a flight attendant when she grew up. About six years ago Don and Alice came back to Eagle for a festivity celebration. I could not believe it when I recognized him as he looked forty years ago. His wife looked young too, she reminded me of the actress, Dyan Cannon.

Charlie and Isaac had a head start in Wrangell, so after a few years in the village school, they were ready to go off to high school in Mt. Edgecumbe, near Sitka in the southeastern part of Alaska. Charlie was about 5'8" and athletic with a quick, Clark Gable smile. Whenever there was a basketball game between Mt. Edgecumbe and another school, we would all sit with our ears glued to the radio waiting to hear the name "Juneby." Since we didn't know or understand the rules, we cheered as "Juneby" makes another point as well as when he fouled. Isaac was taller, probably closer to six feet, slim with Dad's good looks. He was the family brains, with good grades.

19

Back in Eagle, I was struggling with the ABC's in a one room class. One of the things I had to get used to was having to be around other children. Sara and I were very close. She helped me a lot in the class and stuck up for me whenever I got myself in a jam. Sharing with my family was one thing, but with someone else was another.

Ole Hansen was one of the teachers well remembered by my people. She came as a young woman in the 1920's and lived in the middle of the village at the school building in an adjoining apartment type of housing with no modern facilities. There are some good stories told about this marvelous white woman who took to the Indians, treated them with respect and love. She was a teacher and a self-taught nurse. She helped deliver babies as well as teach in the class; a good Christian woman who taught the people about the Lord and always looked to those in need of food or medical care. She and her husband Barney had one son, who is a bush pilot out of Nome, Alaska. They both have gone home to the Lord in the 70's. My memory of them is that they were hospitable to Indians and whites alike. She was tall with a soft, quiet look about her. Her movements were graceful. He was short, stout and always wore an interested, curious look on his face. In the Eagle museum sits her dancing slippers, all beaded and nearly worn out from one too many dances.

One year the B.I.A. (Bureau of Indian Affairs) sent a teacher to the village who was from Los Angeles, California. This was the first black man we had ever seen.

A maintenance man was hired by the school to keep things running. He was the one who made sure there was water, and oil for the stove and generator. The generator was so loud you could hear it all across the village, from one end to another. Our mothers would take turns coming to the school kitchen to prepare hot lunch for us, mostly hot soups, GI surplus crackers and dried fruit. Sometimes the B.I.A. would send some cocoa, the kind you mix with dried powdered milk. No matter how much we hated the hominy, we were forced to sit

20

and eat it under the watchful eyes of Mr. Richardson. He'd make us face the wall for an hour or he shook us by the shoulders. All you could do was hang onto the chair and go for a little bronco riding. There were some good times too. On Friday nights, we had movies at the school or would have lunch box socials to raise money for different projects.

At Christmas the school would put on a program at the "Club House," the local community building where most events took place. The Episcopal Church was decorated with spruce boughs and crepe paper of different colors to make it look festive. Usually one of the Priests or the Bishop would fly in with the mission plane to celebrate the birth of Christ. Bishop Gordon, who was the Bishop of Alaska, came flying over the village with a plane load of food for the Christmas dinner at the Club House. Turkey sure tastes good after a winter of wild meat. *Gee Hee* means Pastors, Preachers, or Bishop.

Sara went to live with Mary Ann and Silas for one summer. I was *lost!* For the longest time I cried myself to sleep since I didn't quite understand why our family was breaking up, with Mary Ann getting married, Charlie and Isaac off to Wrangell and Mt. Edgecumbe. Now Sara, she's gone too.

Through Mary Ann's delightful family, tragedy struck my family again. While they were on relocation through the B.I.A. program in Denver, Colorado, my sister, Mary Ann died of Lupus.

With no phones, the only communication link was the *Tundra Topics* program broadcast by KFAR radio in Fairbanks. Every night at exactly 9:20 P.M., the station would send out messages to the surrounding bush communities. A message went to my parents and to Sophie and Arthur; Mary Ann had passed away in Denver and Silas will be bringing the casket and children home to Eagle Village. It was a terrible blow to them. We were already in bed, but got up when we heard all the weeping and neighbors coming in to visit and help. Mary Ann is buried in the Indian cemetery in Eagle.

Walter was left with Silas, Sophie and Arthur. Regi,

Sophie (*Soot-Toot*) and Billy were placed with a nice, Christian foster family, Leroy and Pauline Krueger. At that time he was a doctor at the Army base in Fairbanks. When they transferred to Wisconsin, with Silas' consent, they took the three kids with them.

Debbie was placed with other foster parents who hadn't enough confidence in the system or respect and consideration for her family; fearing they would lose her, they fled, abducting my lovely niece and raising her in North Carolina. For years, we didn't know where she was. We thought she had been adopted out permanently without any input from her family as often happened to Indian children. In the 1970's another very nice Christian couple in South Carolina figured out that Debbie was a kidnapped child and were able to bring her back to Alaska. In 1976 she was re-united with her family. She is a 'spitting' image of her mother.

Our family's sad experience with Debbie's childhood was common in those days. It is saddening to think back and remember how Indian children were pulled from their villages and placed in non-native homes and simply taken out of the state under the old welfare system. These were the children that have no knowledge of their Indian heritage. Some found their way back to Alaska not knowing what to expect; they have deep culture shock. I have a cousin who was raised in New York. He saw a porcupine and thought it was a raccoon. There's a new law which came into effect several years ago, *The Indian Child Welfare Act*, an act to protect Indian children from being taken from a village or reservation. The Tribal Council has all the power to decide where a child will go in the best interest of the child. Now, every effort is made to place children within the family.

The security I had known with my family all around me was crumbling. I was too young to have strength for myself and my family as we and the people of our community and race were being threatened by change and alcohol. I fought all change because it was the thing I thought was messing up the happy life I had always known. When we moved to Eagle, we didn't know what lay ahead of us and how alcohol would be the major factor in destroying our Indian way of life, perhaps forever. But I fought a losing battle in those days for my childish desires, for my family's survival, for so many things which seemed to be slipping away.

Eagle is 200 air miles east of Fairbanks. It is only 6 miles from the Canadian border on the Yukon River. The Indian Village is 3 miles up river from the city. Eagle was the first incorporated city in the interior. Fort Edgbert, an Army post in the early days, still stands today. In the 70's it was renovated as a museum and has daily tours of the old horse barns and grounds. There is plenty to see. The Eagle Historical Society keeps it running smoothly.

Today, Eagle has grown with stores, post office, restaurants and a hardware store; in the summers the population swells to 175 to 200 people. When I was a child, there were fewer than 60 people in the village and Eagle City had only 10 to 13 residents. The village and city in those days were one big community, having pot lucks and dances together. We would all get dressed up in our best clothes. My best friend and I would exchange clothes like girls do these days. We learned how to do the jig, Virginia reel, two step and square dances to fiddle and guitar, played by the Indian men. The guitar and fiddle music came to the natives when the Hudson Bay fur traders came in contact in the 1840's. Since then, it has been a part of our tradition. Sometimes the dances were not over till the early hours of the new day. One dashing couple, Anton and Esther Merly, came to Eagle during the time the Taylor Highway first opened up, in the 50's. They were from the State of Washington. She was the postmistress and ran a roadhouse. Anton had a generator to provide electricity to the dozen or so in the city. Esther was the one who taught us to do the schottish, polkas and other dances to Anton's accordion. Light on her feet, she was the life of the party. Even if it was 40 or 60 below zero, we danced till our gasoline lamps needed filling while the men kept filling the heater with wood.

One New Year's Eve, my friend and I were standing to the side on top of the benches, watching the dancers. When midnight came around, we heard a lot of commotion going on outside the Club House. Lo and behold! One of the elders and some of the young men came dancing into the hall with native costumes on. They danced and sang to beating drums. This was probably the first time I had heard Indian songs or seen our native dances. I got a little scared with all the noise until I spotted Charlie among the dancers. I could relax and enjoy the performance. I was so proud of Charlie and the others. As I write, I feel a sadness in my heart. All this native art seems long lost, while alcohol remains "alive" and seeking to destroy.

How I used to yearn to go back to the peaceful days of Coal Creek and Woodchopper. It was so different living in Eagle. We didn't have a house. So, for awhile, we lived with our grandfather, Little Paul. He was deaf and reminds me of Mr. Grouch. We didn't dare go near or touch his belongings. But, he had a heart to put up with us. He loved his tea boiled and black, his snuff and visiting with people his age as often as he could. He was always on the go. In the late 50's he died in his cabin with a can of snuff in his hand. God have mercy on his soul!

Alcohol was beginning to make greater waste to my beloved family. We began to see more of a struggle for the necessities, but there was always meat or dried fish on the table if nothing else. We fared better than some, Mom sewed and kept things going.

On my birthday in 1956, Ellen Florence was born in Fairbanks. She was 3 months premature and it was thought she wouldn't live, so Bishop Gordon baptized her the very next day.

There was another baby born after Ellen, but he died one day later from what they call SIDS (Sudden Infant Death Syndrome). We buried him with flowers made from crepe paper. It was a sad and dark day for Mom. At the grave site we all kneeled and cried. Life goes on with summer—fishing for salmon and drying it so we

24

could store it. There was no electricity and freezers to preserve food or hold our goods. Charlie and Isaac were now old enough to go firefighting to earn money to go back to Mt. Edgecumbe in August. Once they pitched in and bought Mom a new set of melmac dishes. You should have seen the twinkles in her eyes. Around this time they helped Dad build a new log home in the middle of the village next to Mom's brother, Charlie. He and his wife had four boys. I used to go help wash the diapers on a scrub board. She treated me good and gave me things in return. She would, on most days, tell me about the stories she read in the True Confessions or True Story magazines. A few times I helped her make pies or cakes in her wood cookstove. Uncle Charlie had a job at Hog River and came home when he could get a few days off. I think he worked at a gold or other mineral mine near Fairbanks. I always thought of her as being well-off by our standards.

During these days, about the time I turned 10 years old, Sara and I discovered *cigarettes*. All the other girls were smoking and in order to be in with the IN crowd or whatever our reason, we began to sneak it. But there was no fooling Mom. She had ESP (Extra Sensory Perception) or something close to it which helps mothers know when their kids are up to mischief. We couldn't hide a thing from her. We babysat or did other chores as punishment for our bad habit. But, the punishment didn't stop us, we were determined. We all figured if we smoked in the church no one will ever know. That was the last place they would suspect, or so we thought. While we were sharing a stub one day, we got caught. Can you imagine what happened next?

Mom's new log cabin was homey with homemade curtains and a new table that Dad made before going back to the mining camps. After working all summer, he bought her a brand new wood cook stove and had a heater made by Ole Hansen's husband. He used a 50 gallon drum to which he did some welding work to put a door on. Today, you can purchase a simple kit to put into the end of a drum and make a *Yukon Heater!* We had that old heater for many years. The cookstove is in my cabin in Eagle.

I remembered the times too, when all the village kids would play cowboys and Indians. We were brainwashed by watching movies where the Indians were always the bad guys killing and raiding the wagon trains. Nobody wanted to be the Indians. We spent a lot of our playtime arguing and fighting about it. The bigger and older kids always made sure they were the good guys. Now that I look at it, we younger ones were the good guys all along! If given a chance to play an Indian part, I would jump at it in a minute. I'm proud, today, of my heritage, culture and for how the good Lord made me. I couldn't act, but I can write. How's that for English being my second lingo?

Since the movie *"Zhur Hee Ch oo dzoo"* (*Dances with Wolves*) came out with Kevin Costner, the outlook on the Native Americans has changed. Many nights I would lay awake wondering how it would be without alcohol in our villages and reservations. There have been cases of child neglect and abuse, families falling apart and consider the countless, senseless deaths. I saw it happen while growing up in my own little village. There will always be denial as long as a person is addicted. They soon look at it as nothing wrong. It becomes pretty much accepted until things get out of hand or cause some heartaches and grief—a person dies from alcohol related car accident and it's called "car accident" but alcohol is never mentioned, out of respect of family or victim. Or a child could burn himself with hot water while the parents are drunk; that's accident? I see it as child neglect. Until a person is ready to admit that he or she has a problem, we will continue to let our Indian culture die out. Our future leaders will be affected by alcohol one way or another. Alcohol is the leading cause of accidents and crime in the United States. If you go to the penitentiaries and jails, full of prisoners, ask any one of them and see what got them where they are today—ALCOHOL. I have members of my family serving time, one got over 20 years. I pray that the Lord will use this chance and my story to bring them around. God can use you in his own way. You may be locked up and have known days when you thought everyone had abandoned you.

God will not abandon you, God does not lie and God does love you! II Peter 3:9 says *"The Lord is not slow about his promise as some count slowness, but is patient toward you, not wishing that any should perish, but for all to come to repentance."* You have a friend and that's Jesus. Have faith and trust Him with all your heart and be on guard. In Ephesians 6:11 the word says *"Put on the full armor of God that you may be able to stand firm against the schemes of the devil."* Remember that there is one more powerful and that is your Jesus Christ our Lord.

The Episcopal Church used to send missionaries to Eagle and hold Bible Schools for us. Two of the missionaries were Reverend Murray Trelease and Reverend Bill Baldridge. Both were single, and always willing to spend time with people of all ages. Rev. Trelease was a pilot, he did all his bush ministry by flying to the villages in the small plane the Church provided for him in Fairbanks. Rev. Baldridge came during the summers. During the short time he spent with the people, he would have overnight parties for us kids at the city parsonage with a big bonfire on the bank of the Yukon River. We had the greatest time roasting hot dogs and marshmallows, then into the late evenings we'd all sit around the fire and he would tell us some scarey stories, not the gory kind you see on television or in movies today.

One night while the girls were getting ready for bed upstairs, the boys decided to sneak up the stairs to spook us. One of the girls overheard their conversation. Sound carried in that house and in the quiet of the night, while pretending sleep, you could hear a mouse scratching for food or the Reverend snoring in one of the downstairs rooms. To counter their spook, we were ready with a couple buckets of cold rainwater. They never tried that again. And, I imagine the Reverend slept through it all because that was the only thing we talked and laughed about the next morning. I don't think the mischief guys

27

thought it was very funny.

Then there was a young couple from New York, Bob and Carolyn Hatcher. They were so sweet to all of us in the village. They were there for the summers too and while there, taught us a lot about cooking, sewing and God's word. On the weekends they would have us down for dinners, picnic and church. I wonder where they may be today. Years later, after we were home for the summer from high school, Rev. Baldridge came back for a visit with a little graying on the sides, tall and handsome. The snoring Rev. was still single and serving the Lord. The last time I saw Rev. Trelease was in Seattle with his wife Mariette and three children in 1968. These missionaries were the ones that taught us the Bible verses and about God. I thank the Lord for sending them.

Winters in Eagle are cold, sometimes temperatures dip to 60 degrees below zero. One has to keep busy sewing beads or leather. Cutting wood is a good way to pass the time or visiting from house to house drinking hot tea or coffee. When it warmed up a bit, we were allowed to go outside to go sledding down the steep bank in front of the village. Some of us didn't have sleds, so we would find an old tin roof laying around. A bunch of us would pile on it. Usually the one in front would end up with the rest of us on top of him.

One night, on a full moon, there was a herd of caribou coming down the frozen Yukon towards the village. Scurrying up the bank and hollering *Wed-Zey* (Caribou), Dad and the men went blasting away with their guns. Going to bed that night, there was a lot of happy, thankful people with tongue soups or roasted heads on their minds.

We had our good and bad times. Our lifestyle was changing so fast, we had to learn to be survivors; looking after the younger ones and fending for ourselves most of the mornings and getting ourselves off to school. This, I believe, made us independent in a lot of ways. Hunger was part of my everyday life now—I would have dreams of our great life in Woodchopper and Coal Creek.

We had to learn how to dress out a caribou or moose at an early age. We had to work for everything we got; forcing a living from the land. Mom made a lot of soups to stretch our food supply, adding biscuits and cakes made from scratch. I can still smell the dried vegetables she put in the soups. It was a treat when she'd put in some fresh carrots and potatoes which she had stored in the root cellar under the cabin. The carrots were just as fresh as when they were picked out of the garden. Dad would fill up a wooden barrel with damp sand, then he would layer the carrots in between the sand. Potatoes were sacked in the gunny sack after they were dry to prevent them from rotting. Indian people have relied on the land for food for many years. Wild game was the main meat source for our diet. Everything from berries to plants were used. Spruce roots from spruce trees were dug up in the spring to make birchbark baskets. The women would split the roots to sew the baskets together. To get a little fancy,the roots were soaked in wild berry juice to color them. Before the Rit dye came out this was the way it was done.

Dad would sit for hours and make snowshoes out of *babiche* (caribou hide stripped into long thin strips to bind the snowshoe together). The older women would make baby carriers out of birch bark. Each carrier would be so decorated up with beads and colored roots you would think it was too pretty to use. If the carrier wasn't used, the babies were wrapped around in a blanket with a beaded strap on the women's back. This way the mother could go about and get at whatever needed to be done around the house. The men would be proud to go out hunting with their beaded rifle case, or to show off their beaded guitar straps at the dances. We were proud people once, living off the land. There were no government giveaways to live high on the hog. Food Stamps is one way to tell the people they can go to the local stores to buy steaks or get fast cash. The government made life easier for the Indian people, but in a way spoiled them by all the giveaways. Then they wonder why we have so many problems in our villages and on the reservations.

Drinking has become the only way of life for my people and the future generations where once proud people worked very hard and were fulfilled with their creativity and resourcefulness. One of the best things that ever happened was when education was stressed upon my people. Without that it would be like losing everything but your soul. Today we have Indian lawyers, doctors, nurses and writers and many other professions. I am not bitter, but thankful for the opportunity the Lord set in front of me.

In the late 50's our youngest brother, Benjamin, was born in Fairbanks. Ben was as cute as a bug in a rug. How we loved and cared for him since he was the baby. Ben was sick a lot. Several times a year, Mom would have to take him to the hospital for pneumonia. We almost lost him a couple of times, but each time he bounced back to a happy, contented kid growing up with all the attention given to him. Ben has two big dimples on each side with dark brown eyes. Like Archie, he grew up tall and lanky, loving fishing and dancing. At the dances, he used to swing us around so fast and hard that we almost fell. Ben lives in Beaver these days with his family. Occasionally he sends me some salmon strips and dried meat called "jerky" in this part of the country.

Ben and Archie were so mischievous, Sara and I would most of the time try to get out of watching them. Once when Ben was about five years old, Archie gave him a knife and he chased us all around the table until we got a chance to grab the knife or run out the door. Of course, he was just playing around, but it sure scared Sara and me. (It was like going through a haunted house for the first time) They threatened us about our smoking if we ever said anything. Years later, we finally told Mom while she was in a wheelchair from a stroke. We thought it to be funny then.

Another time we were left in charge of the house while Mom took her beadwork to town to go shopping. I don't remember exactly how all of this came about. I remember Sara and I forgot to close the cellar door and before we knew it, Ben fell in, headfirst! We panicked thinking

Charlie at Mt. Edgecumbe High School.

we'd nearly killed Ben and Mom would kill us for sure. Ben cried, but was mostly scared and overwhelmed this happened. He got over it eventually, but this, also, wasn't told to Mom until later years.

During the winters, most of the men would trap and then try to find some seasonal work in the other parts of the year. Whether it was firefighting, road commission or working at the gold mines, it was a paying job and they could prepare for the long dark winters that lay ahead. In the fall, the women and kids would go out in the wilderness (woods) and pick blueberries, cranberries or high bushberries which we used to make jelly. You couldn't beat the blueberry pancakes or syrup on a cold, chilly morning! Sometimes we'd sell our berries at the local grocery story to buy some candy and pop. My friend and I used to plant potatoes for $2.00 a day so we could give it back to the store owner for candy, gum and pop. That was a lot of money back in those days.

31

It was in 1959 or 1960 when Charlie graduated from high school. One year following, Isaac (Ike) graduated. How proud my parents were of both of them! Charlie joined the Air Force for five years and was stationed in Lackland, Texas until he was sent over to Turkey for a few years. He was training to be an airplane mechanic and to learn to fly. After the five years were up, he moved to San Francisco where he played basketball for the American Indian Center at 16th and Mission. Isaac was in the Army at Fort Ord, California and stationed in Germany. When he came home after doing his duty, Mom was very happy. She had always favored Ike and missed him very much. Later he went into real estate in Fairbanks and worked for a Native organization.

Charlie and Me, 1970.

3

Chemawa, Oregon

I had just finished 7th grade when I went off to an Indian boarding school at Chemawa, Oregon, five miles north of Salem, the capitol. What a culture shock, going through Seattle, Portland and Salem for the first time! Chemawa was a government school with over 800 Alaskan natives and Navajos from Arizona and New Mexico. It was here that I learned that the Athabascans and Navajos are closely related, even some of our language is the same. It didn't take long before my girlfriends and I were speaking Navajo and dancing Navajo native dances. We'd put on their beautiful costumes and dance the night away. One of the girls, whom we nicknamed "Dixon" was so good at speaking Navajo that she would interpret whenever there was some kind of feuding going on between us. She was from Venetie, Alaska. One of the things I most remember about this nice looking girl with the high cheek bones was that she was quite a hair dresser. She'd fix her hair in a fashion that looked as if she'd just been to a beauty parlor.

One night we decided to get into mischief. I don't recall exactly who all was involved, but my roommate and friend Marty was the leader. She directed, "One of you grab her hat and run!"

It wasn't five minutes until we heard one of the matrons (housemothers) marching down the hall to our room. Knowing we were hiding in our room, she opened the door and ordered us to the main office to face Miss Mitchell. It was like a nightmare whenever we got sent to her office. Miss Mitchell was single and probably in her 60's; short and grumpy, looking through thick glasses. She was *very* strict, to the point that if she thought a miniskirt was too short, she'd embarrass the wearer and tell it like it is!

We were expected to be lady-like at all times, in the dining hall or downtown Salem. There was no smoking in the public or in anyone's homes, except for the designated area at our dorms.

There were a lot of good things about the Navajos. They didn't smoke, practiced their native culture and hung onto their beliefs. They didn't really care who was around, they were always jabbering away in their language. The school wanted everyone to speak English. If we were caught speaking Indian, we would get demerits. If we got three demerits in a week we were not allowed to take part in campus activities on the weekend. We were further punished by having to clean the bathrooms, scrub the halls or do kitchen detail. Kitchen detail included taking responsibilities, learning to cook and keep things clean. It was a STRICT, but a good school. With 800 kids, they had to be strict. Most everyone went by the rules except for little minor things like sleeping in or being late. There was no "hanky panky" in those days. If it had not been for the sexual revolution in the 60's and even today, there would be no such thing as AIDS (Acquired Immune Deficiency Syndrome) I believe this is God's wrath on the human race. Unfortunately, innocent people of all ages are affected—all because of SIN.

Romans 1:18, *"For the Wrath of God is revealed from Heaven against all ungodliness and unrighteousness of men, who suppress the truth in unrighteousness."*

The whole chapter in Romans 1 talks about immorality and in Romans 13:13, *"Let us behave properly as in the day, not carousing and drunkenness, not in sexual promiscuity and sensuality, not in strife and jealousy."*

My first year there, I had to repeat the 7th grade and I missed my home terribly. I was upset, but I guess I just wasn't ready for the 8th grade. I was shy and quiet. I didn't know what to say and felt uncomfortable being there. I froze and looked away fast whenever a boy would talk to me. My second year I was getting used to the system and making a lot of friends. I started to feel more at home. The campus had three dorms for the boys, two for the girls, a gym and a huge dining hall. All the food was good, but there were times when I was missing my native food, especially when mouton (mutton) was on the menu. Some rooms had a total of three girls, other had anywhere from four to six. We had our own closets and bed areas. Overall the rooms were a comfortable size.

Marty and I got involved in sports. Soon we were on the girls' basketball team. One year I was the Captain for the team we put together. We used to play half court and I played the forward position.

Marty was a good player and more like a tomboy, tall and solid with a quick answer whenever we got ourselves into trouble. She was the one we looked up to. Another time we dared each other to run around the gym during the girls' gym night on Thursday. "OK, let's go," was her command! Checking to see if our recreation leader was nearby, off we went racing with the boys yelling out their windows. They made such a ruckus which attracted the girls and our leader in the gym. As we were coming through the door, there stood our Rec leader and some of the dorm leaders. We never tried this again. A few times we would be way back in the line in the dining hall and would plot to get ahead. Whenever we would cut in line to get closer to the serving line, all 800 kids would holler, not in a mean way, but mostly to embarrass us. So that's another dare we wouldn't try again.

There were so many things to do and school was getting harder. But I had already made up my mind that I was going to graduate. No matter how long it took. For three years in a row I took some easy subject for credits such as choir or drivers' training. My last year I took typing. As I got older and wiser, things started getting easier. I even stayed for summer school. Marty and I practiced basketball and went horseback riding for the first time. We went to the beach and swam a lot too.

There was no problem getting off the campus since there were only 25 to 30 of us there. As long as they knew where we were, everything was okay. My sophomore year wasn't too bad. I made it on the junior varsity cheerleading squad. I hated it since I was still on the shy side and was afraid to make a mistake. Although this was not for me, I stuck it out because one of my friends, Sally, was on it too. She was an Eskimo from western Alaska. Of course, there were always guys here, but the ones from St. Paul's Island, Alaska were the best looking of all! They were the Aleut tribe; part Russian with Russian names. One gal, Jane Lind, was very popular. She had a voice and sang at a lot of our school functions. She ran for the student body President one year and while she didn't make a promise in her campaign speech, she said she would *try* to keep the dances going until midnight on the weekends. I believe she got all 800 votes, but the midnight dances never came about. Jane was light skinned, with black hair, a natural beauty. She had her serious look, but a smile that was worth a million. She always said she was going to be an actress and today she is acting successfully in New York. In the March 1991 issue of *ALASKA* magazine, there was an article about her.

After six years, I finally graduated from high school. My senior year was the best of all my years there. I was still playing basketball and feeling more confident in myself. My favorite class that year was Modern Problems with Mr. Donald. This was also my home room. Mr. Donald was humorous and funny, but could be serious too. One other girl, an Aleut, tall with reddish hair, that I especially recall in that class was from Karluk, Alaska. Mr. Donald nicknamed her "Mukluk Mary," she was so outgoing and friends with everyone. Also, the class clown from Hydaburg, Alaska. He was on the football and basketball team and with his good looks, he had a new girlfriend every week. Because of this good looking boy, Sally and I got into trouble passing notes in the class. I cried from embarrassment.

My teachers were mostly white people, however, there

were a few Indian employees on the campus. There were one or two Native American teachers. Charles Evans, an Athabascan from Rampart, Alaska, was a shop teacher. His wife, a Sioux Indian, was my English teacher. Since those years, Mr. and Mrs. Evans have passed on.

It was a great school, even though, we didn't think so at the time. This is where I met my friend Sarah James, from Arctic Village, Alaska. We were roommates our last year, and graduated at the same time. Sarah was a friend who always put others before herself. While the rest of us were acting like a bunch of wild Indians, Sarah was studious, yet fun to be with. Like the time we hid under the beds. Every Sunday night, everyone in the dorms would march over to the auditorium for an evening of entertainment. Well, on this particular Sunday, we decided we weren't going to go. In our rooms under the beds, we got to giggling. Then when a

The year I graduated.

matron came checking with her big, old flashlight; quiet as a mouse! We proved to our friends that it could be done. As I look back, there was no reason at all for this mischief.

Sarah is a native leader for her village and a spokesperson to protect the Caribou herd in the Porcupine area. For many years her people relied on the Caribou for subsistence. When the oil companies wanted to do some exploring a few years back, Sarah and her people fought for their subsistence rights. As one elder said, "We don't eat oil." These indigenous people and their strong leaders got their wish.

After graduating, I spent a few weeks in Fairbanks with my Aunt. She is my Mom's youngest sister. It was a good opportunity to get a summer job and to get to know my aunt better. My first impression of her was that she was so nice, quiet and graceful. My brother Charlie was working for the B.L.M. (Bureau of Land Management). On his days off, he would come out to her house and visit, sharing news and enjoying the native food Aunty prepared when Charlie came. A highlight of our news was our sister Sara's marriage to Horace Biederman, Jr., known as Junior. Junior was half white, a big man once referred to around Eagle as "Cannon." They had a baby girl, Maureen; she died as an infant—more losses in our family.

When I was in Eagle, I was young and innocent, but not too young to try alcohol. This was the night I would have to live with the rest of my life.

Thankfully, I've been healed of all hurt, emotional and physical. There were lots of vodka shots, one after another that night. I vividly remember being thrown around and my clothes being grabbed at—I fought, kicking and screaming, but there was no one nearby to hear my screams, only my physical strength kept me from being raped but the emotional scar has never left my shameful face. I escaped through the cabin door, confused and hurt. Was anyone going to believe me? No, instead rumors were spread like wildfire, no one believed me and people died supporting the bootleggers.

Now that I am healed, I can finally tell my side, leave it behind and go on living the good life.

4

Flower Children / AIM

One day I got a call from the B.I.A. that I was going to be sent to Oakland, California so I could start nursing school in August. The day before I was to leave, Charlie gave me some money to go shopping for clothes. Aunty took me downtown to J.C. Penney's and helped pick out my clothes. All the while I had butterflies in my stomach and was apprehensive about traveling by myself. There were times when I had doubts about this long trip, I had been to Oregon before, but never by myself.

Once there, I met up with some of the kids I knew from Chemawa. Mukluk Mary was one of them and so were others from Hydaburg. One month later, Sarah joined us. I was lonely at first until my friends from Chemawa started getting together on the weekend. Sally was in San Jose going to a beauty school. One day I walked in while she was in class. What a surprise! Months later she got married and was living in San Francisco. Since then, I have lost contact with my little friend, Sally from Eek, Alaska.

The school in Oakland was a four months course of Nurse's Aid training. How disappointing because I applied for L.P.N. (Licensed Practical Nurse) at Chemawa. "There must be a mistake," I told my counselor at the B.I.A. I went ahead and took the course, studying with races of all colors; whites, blacks, Asians, and Indians. I passed with flying colors and when finished, my counselor at the employment agency applied for a grant from CETA (Comprehensive Employment Training Act) for the L.P.N. training. I worked part-time and trained at some of the Bay Area hospitals. During the time I was in training, I got a chance to meet Dean Martin's ex-wife, and I used to see his kids come to visit. Because this was a celebrity family, no one was allowed in the room but the nurses and the doctor. A lovely, elderly woman, with white hair and a soft voice, she reminded me of a cuddly grandmother. But, I never got to meet Dean himself.

[Note: Dean Martin was married three times; his first marriage was to Elizabeth Ann McDonald, 1940-49, there were four children, Craig, Claudia, Gail, and Deanna. His second marriage in 1949 was to Jeanne Bieggers, and they had three children, Dean Paul, Ricci, and Gina. His third marriage was to Cathy Hawn and they had no children. I'm uncertain which wife was in the hospital at this time.]

San Francisco was just over the Bay Bridge, so on weekends, Sarah and I, with our new friends would pile in a car or bus and head for the American Indian Center. There was a trophy in a showcase with Charlie Juneby's name, along with all the other players. I couldn't believe it when I saw it with my own eyes in 1967.

It wasn't too long before Sarah and I hit the hippie scene on Haight Ashbury. Or we hung out at the Golden Gate Park, drinking apple wine or getting high. The flower children made me feel accepted and loved. Whenever we'd go to a temple, they would chant and throw incense all around. The religions they were practicing included Buddhism, Hari Krishna and many more, probably everything but Christianity. If it hadn't been for God's merciful grace, I could have easily been drawn into one of those religions. At the time, I did not know it, but I was one of the chosen few of God. Ephesians 1:4 explains it clearly: *"Just as He chose us in Him before the foundation of the world, that we should be holy and blameless before him in love."* Salvation is by grace through faith. Another quote from Ephesians 2:8 states: *"For by grace you have been saved through faith and that not of your-selves, it is a gift of God."*

During those rebellious years in California, I hardly ever wrote to my parents, fearing that they would find out that I had dropped out of nursing school or that their shy, quiet daughter was turning hip, wearing army clothes and no shoes. My friends and I, when not on Haight Ashbury, used to party on Mission Street not too far from where the heiress Patty Hearst got arrested in the 70's. In the early 70's, she was the kidnap victim of a bunch of radicals from Oakland. My heart went out for her. I, for one, being around radicals in those days, knew what she must have gone through.

It was the time of rebelling against the government. Being a cop hater was one thing, but try protesting against them! They were like ants whenever there was a concert.

I knew from my upbringing that there was a God and He was the one to pray to. Mom and Dad taught us that from the time we were old enough to know right from wrong. What I was doing was not right; everybody around me was dropping out of school. But, I was not totally ignorant, I made my own choices and was responsible for my own actions. I knew right from wrong and I went ahead and chose to drink and get high with the others.

There was some uproar on campuses such as Berkeley where water hoses had to be turned on students. All along the Lord had his loving hands on me and protected me. For He knew someday I would turn away from all of this and that He was going to use me in His own time. The Lord is not slow in coming back as he promised. In II Peter 3:4 it explains it more clearly than I can: *"The seeming delay at Christ's return is for the purpose of allowing more people to repent. But do not let this one fact escape your notice, beloved, that with the Lord, one day is as a thousand years. The Lord is not slow about His promise as some count slowness, but is patient toward you, not wishing for any to perish but for all to come to repentence.*"

Forgetting and forgiving is not any easy thing to do. I
have had to learn to forgive as I have grown in the Lord.
I had a lot of bad feelings toward everybody in general
and especially toward people who drank. They said
things they wouldn't have said had they been sober. And
I took things which they said harder than I would have
if I hadn't been an alcoholic. I was angry at them, myself
and alcohol when I saw what it was doing. I am not
blaming anyone—what I've done or done to myself is all
in the past.

During these times when we were drunk or high, so
we supposedly didn't know what was going on, I was the
victim of a terrible experience—every woman's nightmare. I was suddenly not so high I didn't know what was
going on! I was being viciously attacked and terrified for
my life, sure I would die, sure I wanted to. Later, I was
found beaten on the street. I spent a week in the hospital, miserable, depressed and terrified. Thank God! He
was with me and I came out of it.

During the next year or two, I moved around the
country, usually on a bus. I wasn't brave enough to
hitchhike. I lived in Seattle for about five months with
my Aunt and Uncle until I got enough money to get a
place at the Y.W.C.A. (Young Women's Christian Asso-
ciation). My aunt and uncle may have noticed that I was
a little different and strange, but if they did, they were
too nice to say anything. Pete was Mom's youngest
brother. He served in the Army and fought in the Korean
War. When he came back to the U.S., he settled in
Seattle and worked at the Safeway store as a baker. His
wife, a white lady, was so kind to me. She and I had so
many good times going shopping for their two-year-old
daughter or going to a wrestling match with Pete. I had
the priviledge of watching Haystack Calhoun in one
match. One Friday night she came by and we went up
on the Space Needle. I don't know how I did that, for I
have always been afraid of heights. Later, Uncle Pete
died from pneumonia complications from alcoholism,
leaving behind a wife and three children, one girl and

two boys. He is buried in the Indian cemetery in Eagle. I always had a place in my heart for my Aunt Kaye.

While living in Seattle, I learned from my Aunt and Uncle that Flo Gundrich from Coal Creek owned and ran a nearby delicatessen. On Mother's Day, 1968, we walked into her little corner store. "Hi, Flo," once more! I had to re-introduce myself, but we reminisced about the days in the 1940's mining camps. Flo looked older, and I had done some growing up, but her friendly smile was still there! I enjoyed telling her how I often missed the baked bacon rinds she had given me and how I had never forgotten the flower boxes all around the mess hall which brimmed with pansies.

After working at a convalescent hospital for five months, I decided to move for one reason or another: first to Fairbanks, then back to San Francisco. At about that time the American Indian Movement (AIM) was coming into the spotlight and I wanted to find out about it.

I recall friends asking Sarah and I if we knew the Indians were taking over Alcatraz Island the next week. Sarah commented, "We'd better get all geared up for it." I never got a chance to take part in that demonstration, but my friend Sarah did.

Before the demonstration, a letter and a ticket came for a trip back to Alaska. Mom had Amnesia and was going through a serious head surgery in Anchorage. Getting on the plane that night wearing a light army jacket, sandals and long straight hair, parted in the middle, I was cold and lonely. It was hard to leave my friends behind me and I was missing them a lot. I kept up with the news of their activities on the radio and newspapers in Eagle. I stayed with my parents while Mom was recovering. Ben and Ellen were still at home and we had such fun together. Once I dressed them up in my clothes, put flowers in their hair with strings of beads for a necklace. Both looked like young kids I used to see on Haight Ashbury. Mom and Dad noticed the changes in me, but loved me and stood by me, happy to have me home to help out.

In the evenings, Ellen and I would stay up late with

Mom and sew leather and beads. Mom would tell us stories about the old days and Indian customs. One was of the way older women in the village would isolate a young girl once she got her period, for months at a time until she was ready to be married off. Usually marriages were arranged by the parents, but most of these marriages blossomed into romance. They did not believe in divorce or separation or even know those words.

Under another custom, my people taught a woman she must respect her husband and the younger men and boys of the family. A woman must never step over a man while he is laying down or while sitting on the floor skinning out an animal. She warned that to do these things would bring bad luck. The men are the hunters and the providers, while the women at home go about doing the daily chores of gathering wood and keeping the water bucket full and many others.

5

Two Street - The Pit

In February, hoping to get a job in the hospital or the pioneer home, I moved to Fairbanks. I stayed with my aunt sometimes or with family friends from Eagle.

All this changed when I got in with a crowd that hung out on Two Street (The Pit), an avenue two blocks long jammed with cafes, gift shops, a drugstore, and *bars* from which loud jukeboxes or bands blared noise in your ears. For a native, like myself, it's hard to resist and walk on by after being cooped up in a village. This is where the action was; alcohol, drugs, you name it. Go in a bar, have a drink, loosen up, and you're headed for TROUBLE. *Alcohol* has no respect for anyone, but Indians especially seem vulnerable to its damage. Unless you have gone through it, you will never know or begin to understand an alcoholic. As a child, I fought against the damage alcohol abuse did to my family. As I grew up, I found myself accepting the damage, then trying alcohol myself. The books are right-on when they tell you acceptance and escape are part of the early motivation for using, then abusing alcohol. The abuse turns from a rebellion against discipline, even discipline of one's self, to a love, almost like passion; nothing is better or more important than the alcohol. It seemed as if even as I was moving through these stages of my addiction to alcohol, *when I would pay attention*, I was watching myself from a distance and KNEW what I was doing to myself, but I wouldn't or couldn't stop it on my own.

When I was living in Fairbanks. Dad came to visit

while he waited to go on the pipeline. One day he ran into one of Dr. Patty's sons on the street and invited him back to my apartment. Of course, we didn't remember each other, but he and Dad told some good stories that day. "His actions and manners were of his father's" said Dad.

By this time in my life, alcohol had taken control of my life and those of the other Natives on Two Street. One beauty contestant at a Native convention came in second in the pageant. Now she was training as a salesperson at J.C. Penney's. She once had a dream of becoming the first Alaskan "Miss Indian America." My friend, whom I will call *"Char"* was instead drawn into the whirlpool of Two Street, drinking too much wine. The last time I saw her, she was in the Detox Center, still quite a beauty with her oriental looks. I do not know if she beat the bottle or is still on it.

For a brief time I was married and we had a son, Patrick. Usually known as *Sonny*, my baby was a bounding eight pounder, twenty-two inches long at birth. The marriage didn't work and a year later we were divorced. As soon as it was all settled and I had custody of Sonny, I took him to Eagle, hoping to start a new life that summer. Mom and Dad finally met their new grandson, Sonny, a burly, fat baby with fat cheeks, like a chipmunk. I stayed with my parents and Ellen and I did some housework, washing, gardening, and fishing for a few weeks. We liked to sit under the smokehouse, talking and cooking half-dried salmon over the fire and eating fresh garden lettuce with sugar on it.

Then one day something happened that would change my life forever. Sonny was napping and I was sweeping the floor and listening to the radio. Something caught my eye through the window; coming up the road was Mom and Dad's neighbor. He was a scruffy looking dude, all decked out in a beautiful beaded Indian-tanned moosehide jacket and a cowboy hat that looked like it had been through the wringer. Except it had too much grease and grime on it to have ever been *close* to a washer! I had laid my eyes on my future husband! My

46

first impression of him when he came to the house was, "I'd like to get to know him better."

Later, I learned he was trapping in the North Fork country. From that moment on, some part of me knew I was going to marry this handsome, blue-eyed "White Indian."

He was in and out a lot at Mom and Dad's. Occasionally we would talk because I found he was easy to talk to. The Indians accepted him because he accepted and respected them. He learned to live our lifestyle; ate what we ate, and even had a few beers with the guys. They would later tell stories on how they got a white man loaded.

After the fishing season was over, I moved back to Fairbanks and did odd jobs. For awhile, I worked at the Chena View Hotel as a maid. Hangover was something I was used to now. However, I would sober up, get well and keep working. I had friends who would babysit Sonny, sometimes he would be at Aunty's house. Whenever he was at her house, I knew he was in good hands.

Then the pipeline boom really got going. It seemed a good idea to send Sonny to his father in Noorvik while I worked as a bartender. It was a good paying job, with tips *and* all the booze I wanted. I was partying around a lot. I had a lot of friends, and all the booze they wanted. It was free, so I stuck it out for the summer. I was in and out of jail, once was thrown into a grungy, gross cell which I later found out was the "Drunk Tank." The last time I was in a cell by myself, it was a nightmare. It took three days to dry out with sweats and cold chills, hallucinating that there were mice running all over the place, clinging to me. Or I would dream that there were war planes flying over us and no place to run and hide. On the third day, the jail guard would set me free. Having a hangover and standing before a judge is something I don't recommend, nor any of the above. Two Street was the home "party place" in the summer of 1975.

I received a letter from Aunty; she and Uncle hadn't seen me for over three months and wanted to invite me over for dinner. Bless her heart! She and Uncle loved me and were concerned about me. But, in my mind, by this time, there was no way they or anyone was going to change me. God or no God, no one cared and I was alone to face it. I was sick and saw no where to turn; I was feeling very sorry for myself. I overdosed with pills and alcohol. I lay in a coma in the ICU, (Intensive Care Unit) at the Fairbanks Memorial Hospital. Aunty and Uncle stood right by my side for three days.

It had been several months since Sonny was living with his Dad in Noorvik. He was too young to understand what was going on.

The morning I wrote these memories, tears welled up in my eyes at the pain in those times for me and my family. Today I realize that the Lord had some plans for me and had given me a second chance. In Romans 8:28, we read the Lord has a purpose for everything: *"And we know that God causes all things to work together for Good to those who love God, to those who are called according to His purpose."*

48

6

For Better or Worse

When Mike Potts walked back into my life, he had been working on the pipeline. While waiting for a call from the union to work on the pipeline, he had worked downtown in a bar as a bouncer. All along I had my eyes on him, knowing he was a good provider. Besides, I had always liked him, so we waited for a good time to get together. The next time he came to town for R&R (Rest and Relaxation), I left my job, packed my things and got Sonny ready to try the trapline life once again. One month later I asked Mike to marry me, we were married in the Methodist Church in Fairbanks. I had told the Episcopal priest, "I am an Episcopalian and want to get married." He refused to do the ceremony, instead wanted to counsel us for one month. The priest told me that because of the pipeline and all the money flowing around the country as fast as the oil was flowing through the pipeline, "the pipeline marriages have a high percentage of divorce." But, we weren't prepared to wait, so with a few friends and family present, with borrowed rings we exchanged our vows on August 2, 1975. When I married this man, I didn't know I was marrying his horses too.

September came, and we made a trip to the trapline for a working honeymoon. Mike needed to check the supplies and it gave him a good chance to do some hunting. We left Sonny with my parents for this trip.

Our trapline was 50 miles west of Eagle. It is in a valley below the famous Glacier Peak. There were cabins all

49

along the trail until we got to the main cabin. We had to use a tarp for the first two days to provide shelter. The sharp wind and cold weather didn't help us get things set up easily. The going was hard for me as we climbed the hills, which are actually sub-arctic mountains that reach well above timberline.

The timberline in the frozen north is about 3500 feet elevation. The tops of these mountains are from 4500 to 6000 feet. Once at the main cabin on Eureka Creek, a quarter of a mile from the North Fork River, I felt like I could sleep like Rip Van Winkle. The next morning, while Mike was checking supplies in the cache, I scouted out the place. All around the cabin were tons of blueberries. A little ways back from the cabin was some dried wood and a clearing where a pilot from Eagle could airdrop our gear when we came back for the winter. From our cabin, we could hear the creek and sometimes wolves howling in the distance. Our new winter home was 10x12 feet, with a wooden floor, homemade bench, table and shelves. In one corner sat a little wood heater. On the wall above it were the pots and pans hanging on nails.

There were books of all kinds on mountain men and Indians. I quickly learned Mike was a Louis L'Amour fan. With no gossip magazines around, I even read a few of the westerns. A copy of *Bury My Heart at Wounded Knee* was nearly worn out. I read it once, then later in that winter, I read it again.

After two and a half weeks, it was time to head back to Eagle and our son. The cabin wasn't a bad place to dry out, but I couldn't wait to get back to town so I could party. Alcohol was #1 in my life, more important than my new husband and son. Yet, I loved them both; my feelings for Mike were the same as the day when I first met him. Mike was great with Sonny, taking care of him, spending a lot of time with him. By the time Sonny was four, Mike was taking him fishing, hunting and camping, not easy activities with a toddler. One day after we were married for some time, Sonny called Mike "Uncle." In our Indian way, Mom and Dad had sort of adopted

Mike. Imagine Sonny's childish confusion about their relationship. He needed to ask Mike a question once and started with, "Uncle—Dad—Who are you anyway?" Another time, he watched Mike and I cutting fish at sunset on a cool evening. "Do salmon have beans in them?" he asked when we cleaned out the raw fish eggs.

Around this time, John McPhee, a writer, came for a visit to our house above the village. John was working on his book *Coming into the Country* and we were among the people he visited with to get his story. A spectacled, gentle, quiet-looking man of medium size, John reminded me of a professor on a campus back in the hippie days. In that book are some comments from a couple of heathen who weren't too careful on what they had to say.

Sonny wasn't feeling too well and started to wet the bed which he'd never done before. I took him to Fairbanks for some tests. He had a kidney problem, which the Doctor diagnosed as reflux (a flowing back). He was put on medication for a year, then we were to take him back for more tests. Eventually, the problem was corrected. I called Aunty and Uncle to let them know we were in town. We were always welcome to stay at their big house (later they sold it to move way out in the boondocks). But I kept my distance because they didn't drink and I sure planned to.

Our first year of marriage was hard. Like most marriages, we had our ups and downs. Mike tried hard to keep it together, working hard on the pipeline and trapline and on the fire fighting crews. Living with a liberated woman was hard on him. We lived on fish, moose, caribou, and rice. More fish and rice than anything else, since we couldn't afford too much. But, we *never once* applied for food stamps. Mike made it good and clear when we started that we would not accept any kind of give-aways, which included some new houses which were offered through state revenue monies from the oil. We learned to get by. It was a treat whenever Dad invited us to dinner. God provided and we didn't starve.

Our cabin was 14'x14' with no water, electricity, or any

51

luxuries. I fixed it up with curtains and rugs so it was more comfortable. Mike's mom would send them by mail or bring them along when she and his dad flew up from Iowa for visits. The cabin set along the Yukon River on a piece of ground that Dad had given us. There was gossip around town that Mike had married me for land. But we wouldn't be celebrating our 18th anniversary this year if that was the case.

Both of us were living a sinful life. Having gone through relationships which hurt each of us, we drew closer and closer. Pain bonded us together as man and wife. In Matthew 19:5 the Word says: *"For this cause a man shall leave his father and mother and shall cleave to his wife and the two shall become one flesh."*

So many times I tried to be a good wife and mother, but each time I kept failing. While Mike was on the pipeline, I began to drink again so much that I reached a point where I promised myself I would *never* drink again. Committed to a psychiatric ward to dry out, there were times when I thought I would never make it. I hung onto life and Mike would get me back on my feet, forgiving me and bringing me back home. Each time I was in and out of Detox, I wouldn't stop, but would soon be abusing the bottle again.

Mike's dad, Bud, owned a Comanche 400 plane. Each summer they would fly up and take Sonny fishing around Anchorage. Bud and Sue were a wonderful couple who accepted Sonny as their grandson. By then, Mike had already adopted him legally, so a special bond was built between them.

My mother, Louise, had a stroke and was living in a nursing home in Fairbanks. Dad would make the trip to see her every once in awhile, as often as he could. She was paralyzed on one side of her body, but her mind was good. Not willing to be bound to one spot, she wheeled herself around with her good foot. My kids named her "The Wheels Grandma." They were intrigued and had little understanding of how hard it was for her to move around.

The trapline times were the best. I had to stay sober

and could enjoy my husband and son. It was like reliving my childhood days, only now I had them to take care of. Mike would be gone for three or four days at a time, setting or checking the traps. He wore his moosehide pants, moosehide parka and mukluks. Mom and the "Goodies Grandma" made the pants in 1973. After we were married, I made the parka and mukluks.

On the day he was expected home, Sonny and I would cook up a pot of dogfood with dried fish, lard and scraps; high protein, high fat and good *junkfood* for the cold weather dogs. After these chores were done, I would cook a nice dinner and bake two dried apple pies—one for him

Sonny and me heading out to the trapline.

and one for us. One cold, boring day, I baked bread in a little oven that would set on top of the heater. It was very good to see him home, so he was treated like a king.

To keep busy in the tiny cabin, while Mike was gone, I beaded, sewed leather into mittens or a new pair of mukluks. I made a special pair of moosehide and beaver mittens for Mike. When he and the dogs pulled into the yard one snowy, cold day, I couldn't wait to show them to him. I yelled, "I've something for you." as I ran out to meet him despite the cold.

I was so excited because I had tanned the beaver hide by scrapping all the fat off and soaking and wrapping it in *TIDE* detergent. After it had dried, I had scraped it until it was nice and soft. I was amazed that I remembered the procedure just the way Mom had done it! It's funny how little things like that stick in your memory.

Sonny was taking correspondence courses and I was supposed to be the teacher! Not an easy time for either of us, since I didn't consider myself a teacher. And I'm sure there were times when he didn't either!

He and I took long walks down the frozen North Fork River checking the small trapline we ran together just to help keep ourselves busy. For three months at a time we would not see any other people. We never were sick and I truly liked the solitude. That winter Sonny and I caught four marten and a ptarmigan. For a change of diet, we also set snares for snowshoe rabbits; then we would argue about who would skin our catch! I sometimes did it, and other times he had to when he didn't have homework.

About a week before Christmas, a pilot from Eagle would pick Sonny and me up with all the furs Mike had caught. Mike would follow, mushing the dog team and bringing other equipment. Dad would be waiting with a homecooked meal, fresh fruits and some good old junk food. I found out fast that my system was not used to the fruit, candy, pop, etc.; it usually took a week before I could handle them again. We'd give Mike two or three days to mush his dogs in to town. During the delay, I could party, which made me so sick I would stay away from alcohol all during the Christmas holidays.

We had packages from Mike's folks, relatives and friends waiting for us. I especially enjoyed reading all the mail that was piled up in the post office. And sometimes read until I fell asleep, then I woke up to a crackling fire in the heater, the smell of fresh coffee perking on our burner propane stove along with eggs, bacon, hashbrowns and toast for breakfast. After three months of eating wild meat, dried potatoes, or meat

Sonny with some Marten

gravy with rice, there was no complaining. Life back in Eagle was great, especially to see Dad in his cabin cooking a pot of stew and making bread.

Of course there was alcohol around. Eagle was considered a "dry town." In the past there had been a liquor store, which was open only certain hours, and the owner controlled the amount of liquor he sold to the people in the village. When he died in 1967, it didn't take long before bootleggers moved in and any kind of control disappeared.

By this time, Mike was very bummed out about my drinking; it took his best to take care of Sonny and help keep me straight. There was no way any other person was going to stop me!

During the summers, we would go firefighting or fishing for salmon. Fishing was one thing I'd look forward to. The first few days, I would cut the salmon belly part of the fish and debone it. Then I could cut it into strips, slicing on the slant so the meat would dry easily. Once the slicing was done, I would soak the strips in salt brine for an hour, rinse them once more then hang them in the smoke cache. I usually hang the fish for a day, until it's half-dried. Now, for the best part, sticking some in the oven until good and crispy. I would put the rest in plastic bags and freeze it.

Much of our summer was spent preparing for the winter, just as when I was a little girl. Whenever the cranberries and blueberries are ready, a bunch of the ladies would get together and pick to their heart's content! All the berries were good frozen or made into jelly.

A few times, for a little cash, Mike and I drove out along the highway to cut firewood for local residents. There was a bar about 30 miles from Eagle, so I was willing to go and help out. Each time, I would get sick, over and over again. Mike would drink a few beers, but from my viewpoint he was only a social drinker. There were times when he would over do it too, but he never kept on going at it like I did.

Mike was in a union, so he got back to the pipeline to work. Once he was in the same camp with Dad. They made friends with a young man from Berea, Ohio and invited him to come to Eagle to visit. The guys would all go to Dad's room at the camp and listen to his stories about trapping and mining. Everywhere Dad went, he was well-liked by young and old alike.

When I found out I was pregnant, Mike came home before his time was up for R and R. He left the pipeline and came back to Eagle and the trap line for us. The Lord used the things I learned through my job at the health clinic about alcohol abuse and pregnancy and He gave me the strength to leave alcohol alone while I was pregnant.

I was about 2 1/2 months pregnant when we mushed our dogs to our little paradise. Sonny was five years old, almost six. He rode in the toboggan most of the way, so I walked most of the time. The Doctor had said I was in good health, but they encouraged a lot of exercise. Walking up the frozen Mission Creek, I thought, "I'm getting my exercise, alright!" After awhile though, Sonny decided he'd had enough of being in the toboggan. He was packed in so he couldn't see where he was going. He

Our lead dog Oddball with a dead Caribou.

started to yell and cry on the top of his lungs, "I want to get out and walk!" To keep him warm against the blowing snow and cold, we had tied the sleeping bag down with him inside. That wasn't going to keep him down. Somehow in the middle of all his yelling and screaming, he wiggled himself out. I was standing on the back of the toboggan when all of a sudden he said, "Mom, I'm wet!" That got him some action fast!

After three months of trapping, Mike left to go back to work on the pipeline and I stayed at our cabin or at Dad's. Mike had been gone for about six weeks and I was about seven months along, when we decided to meet at Fairbanks in May so I could be checked by a Doctor. One day before I was to meet him, there was a message over the radio telephone in town that Li'l Johnny was in the hospital.

A short time later, he died of a head injury from being beaten on a Fairbanks street. It was ruled out as foul play, investigations were closed and to this day, no one knows who beat our Li'l Johnny except for the person who did it. I pray that the Lord will give me the love and

Mike, Ben and Sonny in our trapline cabin.

compassion to forgive this person. If that person ever came to me one day, it would be hard, but Jesus forgave me. Just so we must forgive others and hopefully through prayer and witnessing, lead them to the Lord.

I John 1:9 says: *"If we confess our sins, he is faithful and righteous to forgive us our sins and to cleanse us from all unrighteousness."*

Johnny was the smallest of all my brothers. He learned how to play the guitar and often accompanied Dad on the fiddle. His Indian name was Neen Boy. What Neen means, I don't know, but there was a special meaning from it for Mom and Dad. He was a daredevil and did things like climb the steep cliffs across the Yukon in Eagle during the most dangerous time of the year— spring break-up! With melting snow, slush and no good footing, Li'l Johnny proved to the whole village he was not a little runt. Once we ran home to tell Mom, "Johnny is climbing the cliff." She hurried out, yelling her head off for him to get down. He turned, waved and continued on his journey.

Mom came home from the nursing home for the funeral and I could only imagine what she and Dad must have been going through. Being seven months pregnant, my child was already a member of the family, and the thoughts of their loss was overwhelming. I held up pretty good, so Sonny and I went ahead to meet Mike. Two days later, we all came back to Eagle and buried Li'l Johnny. I could see the pain in Mom and Dad's eyes, but for the umpteenth time, Dad told the story of when Li'l Johnny was born on the airplane.

Near my due date of June 29, I returned to Fairbanks to await the birth of our baby. Sue and Bud came to see us there while I was waiting. My niece Regi came for a visit from Wisconsin. Everybody was waiting patiently, but after a month in Fairbanks, our cash was running low, so Mike went to fight a forest fire. Then Sue and Bud had to return home, as did Regi. Still no baby! I stayed with Grandma Sophie Stevens—waiting. Two weeks overdue, I finally gave birth via caesarean section on July 12 to an 8 lb. 4 oz, 22" baby girl! With her big eyes and cheeks, she looked like a doll you would see in the gift shops. The B.L.M. (Bureau of Land Management) got a message to Mike on the fire site. It wasn't until a week later that I handed him this little bundle of joy as he stepped off a plane. We named her Jody Ann, after Mike's aunt in Des Moines.

I was happy taking care of Jody Ann and Sonny; I did good for the longest time. It was like playing house all over again. Sonny was having a great time with his new sister. He was so protective and would panic if she coughed or spit up the milk. That winter the kids and I didn't go out to the trapline. Mike and Bill made trips out instead. Bill was the friend whom Mike and Dad had met when they worked on the trapline.

We enrolled Sonny in school and, around that time, I got a parttime job at the village clinic as a Community Health Aide. I later got more training and and my certification. The job has the same duties as a nurse practioner under a medical doctor's orders via phone from Fairbanks. I used to take Jody Ann with me on the days Mike was cutting firewood, making runs to the

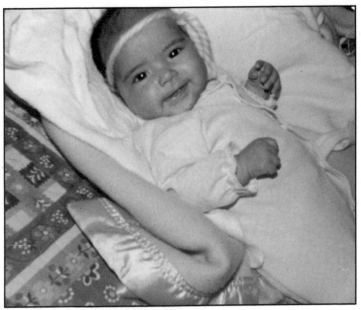

Jody Ann

trapline or mushing his dog team.

At our one room cabin, I sewed, cleaned, baked, and cooked for Mike and the kids. Mike hauled water from the river for baths and for my gas operated wringer washer. He bought me the washer when he worked on the pipeline and it sure beat doing laundry by hand. Washing was still difficult, though, and after awhile we ordered Pampers by the case from a wholesale store in Fairbanks.

My brother Ben and Sonny with a Wolf we caught.

7

Hearing the Word

During that winter, we had visitors from Eagle City. A man and his wife, who were Christians, came to our house. I knew who they were; they used to buddy around with Mom and Dad in the village. Dad liked his company, for he was a good listener and a quiet man. His wife chattered like a magpie, but Mom had always talked good about her. At first, I didn't want them around, but Mike was enjoying him and, after all, they were friends of Mom and Dad. It took me awhile to get close to her. I felt threatened and I didn't want to change. I didn't make any effort to visit her and ignored her whenever I met her on the street or in a store. With their love and patience, they kept coming back. This couple had two boys; one the same age as Sonny. Before long the boys became good friends. Later, they had to go out of town and asked us to watch the boys while they were gone. They were good kids and used to tell Sonny about the Lord.

Towards the end of the year, I found myself getting bored and "DRY"—there was no alcohol in my system and I had a craving for it. That old Satan knew he had me in my weakest point and he would use anything or anybody to get me started drinking again, no matter how hard I tried to stay sober.

James 1:13-14 says: *"Let no man say he is tempted by God.*

"For God cannot be tempted by evil and He Himself does not tempt anyone. But each one is tempted when he

63

is carried away and enticed by his own lust."

The village council told me there was a meeting or a training pertaining to my job in Fairbanks. Here was my chance! Once again, I was "on the bottle" and ended up staying in Fairbanks close to Christmas. Only one week before Christmas, Mike packed up the kids and came into Fairbanks, so I sobered up and we spent the holiday with Aunty and Uncle. It was fun to be with Mom, Dad and Ben there too. Dad came back to Eagle with us.

The rest of the winter was spent keeping busy at work and at home. We did a lot of visiting for we didn't have TV to keep us at home and glued to it. Sewing was a good

Our House in Eagle.

way to pass the time, so once a week the ladies would get together in the village to sew and exchange ideas. We liked going to the "Goodies Grandma's" as she was quite a cook and there was always fresh cookies, pies or pastries served with tea or coffee.

Then, the Christian couple, Steve and Sharon, started coming around more often. Mike and Steve were getting to be good friends. Sharon and I got closer, I even went to the Ladies' Retreat in Tok.

A time came when Mike wanted to mush out towards the trapline and he asked Steve to come along. One night in a little cabin, Steve started talking about Christianity and everything that went with it. Mike was NOT ready to hear about it!! Here in a little cabin was a Christian and an atheist. Mike was so mad, he stormed out of the door. Steve waited for him to return, full of patience and love, just like his wife. I had noticed this couple was happy and really nice, compared to my feelings as there was still a lot of hate in me. Although I was married to a white, I wasn't overly friendly with them. Distrust was great because of all the times I had been hurt. At the time, I did not realize how I had hurt others through my foolishness—my parents, my kids, Mike, Aunty and our only Uncle, who gave so much up to help us. As I look back, Uncle only meant well when he used to talk to us about drinking.

Mike's folks were well known in Eagle. They came in and out in their plane to visit. If there was anyone that I would like to be similar to, it would be Mike's mom. She is so sweet and fitted right in helping out in our cabin. I saw her as a good example—a Christian woman and a good wife. Our daughter, Jody Ann, looks a lot like her these days.

Mike and his dad would be gone for days hunting caribou or moose. When they got back, they had either a caribou or a moose. It would take us pretty close to three days to clean, wrap and freeze the meat.

It was great that Bud and Sue came up to see Sonny and Jody Ann growing up, taking home movies of them and of our lifestyle.

In June, 1978, we were awakened at 3:00 A.M. by a knock on the door. The kids were sleeping soundly and we were careful not to wake them. Our oldest brother, Charlie, was in a car accident between the village and the city. My friend, whom I had grown up with, was the primary health aide and she was called at her home. She chartered out of Eagle to Fairbanks with my beloved brother hanging onto life. Before they made it past the

Glacier Peak, he died from internal injuries. We learned of his death later when we made a phone call from the clinic to the hospital. I was screaming and going to pieces until Mike and a friend, another Sharon, got a hold of me. Sharon was a Californian Indian—married to one of the guys from the village. She was a dear friend and loved by our people. Dad adopted her as one of his own.

Archie was in Eagle, but today both he and Ben were fire fighting. Isaac was in Fairbanks working. He had to break the news to Dad, then with Aunty and Uncle, they went to the nursing home to tell Mom. I heard Dad was in shock, so he went to drinking, but he was not on it too long.

As a family, we all drew close to be strong for Mom and Dad. Sara, Junior and their kids made plans for a potlatch. This is a tradition in our custom for those who pass on. Sara was an excellent cook, so she was more or less in charge in that department. All of Eagle came to pay their last respects to Charlie. An Indian lady from Fort Yukon cried, "Goodbye, Twoshirt." as she headed back to her cabin in the village. She had given him that nickname which had stuck with him until his death. We laid him to rest in the same cemetery as our sisters and brothers, Mary Ann, Margaret Carol, Li'l Johnny and baby John.

A month later, after all was over, the United States Air Force sent a real nice headstone for my brother.

Grieving, that summer I drank more than ever. But the pain was still there.

Mike loved me and I was the mother of his kids, but sometimes he almost gave up on me. He never did completely, Thank God.

Our summers were too short, the time seemed to go by so fast. Usually, the hottest it got was in the nineties, pretty close to 100 degrees. There were a few forest fires the guys and gals went on. During the season, Mike and I would get a baby sitter so we could go on a couple. It was good money, but hot and dirty. When my niece, Regi, came from Wisconsin for a short visit, she got a chance to go on one fire with us.

We noticed Bill was hanging around our house a lot more while Regi was visiting. I told Mike, "He's got his eyes on my niece." We mentioned it to her one day and her comment was, "I only go out with guys that look like Robert Redford." Bill was tall, slim and good-looking. His hair, almost the color of the sun, was shoulder length and he wore a black rim hat, given to him by one of the Indian guys in the village. Mike and I just smiled at one another and let time take its course!

In August, when it was time to get things ready for the trapline, we used our money made on the forest fires to buy some of our supplies, groceries, dogfood, winter clothes such as shoe paks, gloves, socks or long johns.

Mike's trapping was good during the three months we were on the trapline. This was Jody Ann's first year in the bush, but by now Sonny and I were used to it and knew how it was to do without the everyday necessities. There were times when we would get the cravings for candy, Pepsi and gum! I now brought a bunch with us, but we always ran out a month before going back to town. Popcorn was one thing I made sure we had enough of.

When we got back to Eagle, in December, Mike's folks got us some tickets to go to Iowa for the holidays. This is the first time we will get to meet Mike's sister, Cindy, and the rest of the family. Sonny was excited about his first trip out of Alaska, but Jody Ann was still a baby and didn't quite understand what was going on. Mike's sister was out of college and working to buy a condo. She was tall, slim and quite a beauty; the kind that would make it as "Miss America." Sonny had a time of his life! He took swimming lessons and learned to roller skate. Jody Ann was another story—she kept us on our toes and earned her nickname as the "White Tornado." A few times we caught her sticking her head into the toilet bowl or drinking water out of it. One day we searched the house for her, finally she came out of her hiding place; the fireplace! It was good to be in the midst of this wonderful family; the family who stood by us, loved me and accepted me even when they knew I had a problem.

Camping on the way out to the trapline,
with Jody Ann and Sonny.

They were a big encouragement and were supportive through all the dark times. They were the ones who taught me how to love again by loving me without reservation. I owe them my life.

My youngest sister Ellen was now married and living in Fairbanks. She was a good wife and mother; she named her son James Barr Fraser III. One night she got a shock of her life; her husband wanted a divorce, then he took their baby back to Michigan. It was downhill

Gram, Gramps, Mike and Cindy. January 1979.

from there for her. She best described her situation in her story to the Fairbanks newspaper one year, "Loneliness is the deadest anyone can get."

Ellen has regained her life and is now in her 9th year of sobriety. About five years ago, she reunited with her son, James. Now, sixteen years old, he is as tall and handsome as his dad. Actor Christopher Reeves reminds me of Jim. Four or five years after divorcing Ellen, Jim contracted cancer. He received the Lord before he died.

Today, Ellen is married to Mel Rada from White River,

South Dakota. Mel had come to Alaska during the pipeline boom. They have a home in Eagle, but have been living in Fairbanks for four years. He is a self-employed truck driver. "Alcohol Free" is Ellen's motto as she rebuilds her life and tries to help others with alcohol problems overcome them. I admire her for her strength and ability to help others.

In the spring of 1979, Mike, the kids and I went to a ratting camp on a lake near Fort Yukon. We wanted the muskrats for meat and for hides to sell. Muskrat tastes somewhat like domestic rabbit. While we were there, the ice on the Yukon River was breaking up, moving down from Dawson City, Yukon Territory, Canada. One cool evening, I was sitting in our 10x12 wall tent enjoying the warmth of the little camp stove and candlelight. The kids were tucked away for the night in warm sleeping bags, but Sonny was still awake listening to the radio station KJNP on our little radio we carried with us whenever we went camping. It had an antenna that you tossed up in a tree for better reception. Earlier in the day there had been broadcasts of flood warnings for Eagle, but we were busy skinning out the muskrats and

Ice breakup on the Yukon River.

Sonny in front of our tent camp.

ducks and didn't think much about it. Now the announcer came on loud and clear, "To Mike and Adeline Potts from Dad Willie Juneby in Eagle. We had a flood and you lost your house. The dogs are okay."

Mike was out on a lake canoeing and shooting at the muskrat, so we decided we'd better stay up until he got in. Sonny started crying, mentioning the new bike we bought him the summer before with the fire fighting money. Then I started crying, thinking of all the things we might have lost; my new washing machine, half of a moose hide, my yearbook, the list went on until I realized that everything can be replaced but my pictures. While I cried, I recalled the bedroom Mike and Bill had added onto our cabin before Jody Ann was born. Ellen and I had picked moss for insulation to put between the logs; that was the way Indians did it ever since I could remember. She and I weren't too happy with the results. "Next time, we'll buy whiteman insulation," was a statement I made to Mike.

A week after the flood, a plane from Fort Yukon came

to the camp to pick Jody Ann and me up. From Ft. Yukon we caught another airplane to Fairbanks. On the 18th of May, Isaac got married to Sandi. She is an "outside native" and raised in a different part of the "lower 48" than we had lived in. Before she came to Alaska, she lived on a reservation in South Dakota, so she knew a lot about our Indian culture. Now the village gossip buzzed. "Another white marrying into the tribe," was the way John McPhee's book *Coming into the Country* expressed the tale carrying. Some Eagle City folks and the Eagle Village natives were bickering about each other, saying things that were not very nice, including myself. For a small town, there was a lot going on which we didn't know about, but which we babbled about anyway. But, our family welcomed Isaac's beautiful bride and their lovely wedding was a happy time for us. At the reception, we danced to the old time fiddle music played by Dad. Isaac couldn't have picked a better daughter-in-law for Mom and Dad. They were so happy for him. Together, Isaac and Sandi raised three of her teenaged kids and an adopted daughter, Christy.

After the ratting camp, we returned to Eagle and lived in a 12'x14' frame tent with an outside kitchen while we got busy cleaning up the flood mess. Mike's folks came up to help. The kids dubbed Bud and Sue with the pet names of "Gramps" and "Gram." Gram watched Jody Ann and Sonny, while Ellen, Gramps and I cleared brush at the site where we were planning on rebuilding. Old Gramps outworked Ellen and I. Gram did the cooking 'in' my outside kitchen on a little cook stove. Mike took some time off from the clean-up to go fire fighting so we would have some cash to help us recover our losses and keep on.

After Mike came home from fire fighting, Gram and Gramps left for a quick fishing trip around Anchorage. They had to make this a short trip and return to Des Moines to get ready for Cindy's wedding to Dave Cyganiak in October. We missed this humongous, fairy-tale celebration because we had to get things done in preparation for going on the trap line.

Because of a desire to drink that 4th of July, I drove out on the highway and went off the road. I fell out of the truck and rolled down a 15 foot embankment. No one else got hurt, but I came out with a couple of broken ribs. Ellen and another lady from the village were with me. Thank God! They were not hurt. But, drunk as I was, I soon felt the pain from my ribs. I straightened out the next month or two, working hard helping Mike with the new house. He was always so good to me, having hopes of helping me get my life together. Whenever I was sober, I took good care of the kids and did everything with Mike. I even went to church *if* I felt like it; Christmas, Easter or special holidays seemed good enough attendance! I took Holy Communion when it was offered and I had been baptized as an infant. I always knew there was a God because that was the way I was raised. What I didn't know was that I had never received the Lord personally, in my heart, as my Savior. Had never truly believed he was the Son of God and that He forgives all your sins if you confess His name as Savior. There was more to God than a few Sunday mornings each year according to some Christians at Eagle Bible Chapel. There was believing and accepting the Lord.

Down and out after a few days of drinking, I dreaded going to pay a bill where I knew the lady receiving my money, Sue, was a member of the church. I was very careful what I said around her family; I respected this nice Christian woman and wanted to make a good impression on one of the people who explained the plan of salvation to me for the first time ever.

I got through the bill paying experience and continued my life as it had been. But in the back of my mind, this thing about salvation kept popping up. I wanted so much to be like the Christians in town with good, happy homes, yet I was so very attached to my drinking friends and the parties. Praise God, I was beginning a period of being double minded as the Holy Spirit was drawing me to the Lord; I was getting uncomfortable with my life as it had been. The day was coming when I could cross over to the side of God and leave my sin filled life behind me, rejoicing in the freedom of being a new creature in the Lord protected and directed by His love.

That fall, Bill and Regi got married! Little did Mike and Dad know when they had invited him to Eagle that he would marry our niece. She had her Grandpa play the fiddle at her wedding reception and we danced till we dropped. And that I did when I got loaded! There was an elderly lady of over 100 years old who did the jig with half of the village! They used to call Bill "the blonde boy from the village" or "Wild Bill from over the hill." Bill and Regi have three children, Shyanne, Conan and Shawna.

Raised in Wisconsin, this new bride almost poisoned her new husband. She accidentally put a tight lid over a pot of beans with tomatoes in it without having a refrigerator or a place near to keep it cool. The food became poisonous, of course. How was she supposed to know, being that she was new at all of this?

We were still kind of primitive back then; no electricity, phone, TV or plumbing. One time Regi poured Karo syrup into my gas operated wringer washer,

Sonny and I walking out to the trapline.

74

thinking it was Clorox.

"This gal had a lot to learn," I thought. Now Regi can sew mukluks, mittens and make a beaded fringe moose-hide jacket.

Like Mike and I, Regi and Bill had the trapline fever. They made a fine couple. One year, we all went out to the trapline with our kids. They were about 30 miles up the North Fork by the Gold Run. Just two weeks before Christmas, Mike was out checking the line for two days and I wasn't expecting him until the third day. I tucked Sonny and Jody Ann into bed after washing them up and enjoying a little dessert with them. It looked like a good quiet evening to lay back, read a western and listen to the radio station KJNP. The mice were scratching around for food; I think I caught three that night in some mousetraps we brought from Eagle.

Suddenly there was a pounding on the door! We would usually hear Mike pulling into the yard with the dog team, but I hadn't heard anything this time. "Who's there?" I yelled. My heart was pounding so hard I could almost hear it. My first thought was for my loaded 30-30 Winchester. When I heard Regi laughing and yelling back at me to "Open up," it was a real relief. After 3 1/2 months, we had a lot of catching up to do. The cigarettes she brought sure tasted good; I had run out two weeks ago. But, where would I put my guests for the next couple of days. Our cabin was only 10'x12'. The company was worth the crowd though and we managed until Mike got back. Then, he and Bill set up a wall tent outside our cabin where Regi, Bill and Shyanne would snuggle up to keep warm. In the mornings they would make a dash to the cabin for a hot cup of coffee and Mike's famous cowboy steaks. He would chop each steak on both sides, then roll the meat in a flour mix and some dried fruit for a treat.

Mike and Bill spent two days snow shoeing and packing down the snow on the North Fork River, so that a plane could land.

Bill and Regi had made arrangements with the pilot to pick her and Shyanne up in September when they

Jody Ann and some of our winter's Caribou meat.

went out to Gold Run. Two or three days later, she flew back to Eagle while Bill mushed his dog team into town. *This is the girl who was raised in a home with a butler, housekeeper and some gourmet meals.* A few days later, the same pilot came to pick up the kids and I. When Mike made it to Eagle with his dogs, we'd all gather at Dad's house for a big feast and his freshly baked bread. Dad was always known for his warm hospitality, sometimes he would play the fiddle for his grandchildren or tell stories to Mike and Bill for half the night.

For Christmas, we went to Iowa. On the way, we stopped in Fairbanks to visit our families and shop. There would always be the alcohol available, but whenever Mike was with me, I would never continue to drink the next day or drink any hard liquor like whiskey. So, I did pretty well at staying sober, just drinking beer; not admitting that I was hooked on it. Mike was not exactly an angel himself, but we knew the Lord was dealing in our lives through the Christian radio station at North Pole. Praise the Lord for Don Nelson and his crew. The people who live out in the bush would know what I am talking about. Most radio stations have a lot of interference and static. But this one station, KJNP, would come in loud and clear.

We returned home from Iowa while Bill and Regi were still in Ohio. Isaac and Sandi made their home in Fairbanks, after Christmas Ben was in Fairbanks on R & R. Archie was out in North Pole at Uncle and Aunty's house while waiting to go to work. Sara and Junior had Willard and David home in Eagle, while their daughter, Corrine, was in Tok, going to high school. Ellen was in Eagle too, and we were anticipating the same routine for the rest of the winter. I was on call right away at the clinic.

Two days after we got home, Dad was out walking in the evening when he slipped and fell. I was called at home to come down to the village to check it out. Mike and I ran all the way to his house. All out of breath, we found Dad sleeping and could not waken him. After taking his vitals and filling out the S.O.A.P. forms, I talked to the doctor in Fairbanks. He advised me and the other Health Aids to start an I.V. and to medivac him to the hospital as soon as possible. At 10:00 P.M., a plane landed with flares all along the airport. The men from town had come up with flare lights and set them on both ends of the runway. Whenever an emergency came, the whole town came together and helped.

On the way, I kept turning Dad onto his side and talking to him. I was crying inside and praying for Dad. Yes, I needed the Lord and I was crying out to Him. We called the family to the I.C.U. ward; Isaac, Sandi and their kids, Margie, Lisa, Christy and Eddie, Uncle and Aunty, Archie, Benny, Sophie, Billy, Walter and Debbie. Many friends were also standing by our side. Our dear and faithful friend, Cathy Ipalook, from Tok, was one of them.

The next morning, Sandi, Isaac, Mike and I broke the news to Mom that Dad was brain dead and there was nothing the doctors could do for him. In her wheelchair, she came to the hospital and kissed Dad goodbye. She came back to the waiting room and these were the exact words as I remember them: "Let him go."

On the third morning, they pulled the life support

system from Dad. We were devastated! Grief stricken, we went back to the nursing home with Mom, then to Isaac and Sandi's to comfort one another. If it hadn't been for Mom ,being as angry and hurt as I was, I probably would have gone back to drinking right there and then. Watching Mom hold up pretty well, you could see she was a strong believer in the Lord. Once again, we pulled the family together for a funeral in Eagle Village. Regi and Bill came home early from their vacation.

This death was a great loss! I look forward to the day when the Lord comes back as He promised, so we can reunite with our loved ones forever. Some years earlier, in the 70's, Mom and Dad had received the Lord as their personal Savior in Glennallen. It is comforting to know that Dad will be waiting and holding the door of Heaven open! I am also anxious to see if he finally met his hero, John Wayne.

We held our traditional potlatch, a type of covered dish dinner with moose meat, caribou, fish, turkey and roast beef. Chief Andrew Isaac of Dot Lake came. He and Dad

Chief Andrew Isaac in Eagle.

were of the Raven Clan and were cousins in our Indian way. They were that close. He gave a speech, then the family gave gifts to visitors. Laura Sanford, who is a sister to the Chief flew in from Tok, also. Andrew was the traditional Chief for the whole region of the Tanana Chief Conference. He and his office are highly respected and to be compared to the Queen of England or the President of the United States.

Regi and Bill's daughter, Shyanne, once said, "I miss Grandpa and I am hungry!" She was upset and crying at the time.

With Dad gone, I tried to put my life together. Now I was angry at God, if there was a God! "Why?" was my question so many times. Steve and Sharon came and visited us, had us over for dinner a few times and comforted us. She was very patient, not knowing that someday the Lord was going to use me to comfort and to serve Him.

In March of that same year, my favorite little nephew, Conan, was born. Regi and Bill were a happy couple, so why couldn't I be? In December, Isaac and Sandi's daughter, Lisa and her husband were blessed with a baby boy on Dad's birthday. They named him Willie.

Carrying around all the hurt was more than I could take, so it didn't matter if I lived or died. I loved my husband and kids, but figured God would probably take them too, so who cares!

When I woke up in a Detox center, suddenly aware of my condition, I had an awful urge for a beer. Hearing that Mike and the kids were going to church in Eagle while I was taking treatment didn't relieve my depression. This stayed with me when I was dried out; my problems hadn't been solved by alcohol or by losing alcohol.

Experts today tell us alcoholism is a disease, a sickness like cancer or other major disease and there is no cure.

I believe it is a disease and I also believe that our Lord can heal; He did it for me!

I've tried Alcoholics Anonymous (A.A.) and other alcohol treatment centers and I've been through Detox more than once. But, the strength of the Lord's love has

79

delivered me from alcoholism. One of the verses I went by while struggling to stay sober was in Phillipians 4:13 *"I can do all things through him who strengthens me."*

Some say "once an alkie, always an alkie." But, I also believe I am a new person.

Later, I started going with them. After going a few times, something clicked and I wanted to know more, especially about God's love. All this time, He was showing me His love through the Christians in town. Everywhere I went, there they were—the Postmaster John and his wife Betty, store owners Sue and Ralph, the bus drivers John and Sally, and our friends Steve and Sharon. I was now cornered.

Sometime during this period, I received the Lord as my personal Savior, but I still felt I wasn't good enough to be a Christian. Even though I was going to church, I was still doing things that I should not have been doing. I was slow in growing in the Lord and not strong enough to say no whenever there was a party. But with each fall, I asked forgiveness and got back on my feet. And, God, in His merciful love, was building me and filling me with a longing for His ways, helping me to get away from the past and from the guilt of my disappointments to my family and people which I held against myself. I am no longer that old person, but a new creature becoming more and more eager and willing to be led of God and to serve Him and to enjoy His blessing. II Corinthians 5:17 says: *"Therefore if any man be in Christ, he is a new creature: old things are passed away; behold all things are become new."*

It took another tragedy to straighten me out and get right with God. This was the hardest of all the deaths. My younger brother, Archie, took his own life while drinking. He took a 30-06 rifle to his head. The neighbor next door heard the gun shot, but it was too late by the time they got to him. Mom had to come home again for the funeral and potlatch. There was such a feeling of failure and hopelessness. No answers for the questions asked. Our kids were all weeping, for it was too hard for them to understand in their childish ways.

Archie was one of a kind and always full of mischief. As he got older, he never quit growing, he was over 6'2" tall. He could play the guitar by ear and whenever there was a dance, you could count on him to show up. He loved fishing for grayling and setting snares for rabbits. He used to take Sonny to set the snares for rabbits by using #3 picture wire. That way the rabbits won't break the wire and get away. Sonny and Jody Ann loved eating the head. Back when we were children and still today, Indians clean and soak the guts to fry them. This may sound a little gross to some, but to us it was good and nutritious with no preservatives and cholesterol. It is good healthy food.

We will never know why he did this, but looking at it today, I'd rather not know. This was not Archie's way; he may have been depressed by the alcohol and this impulsive act destroyed him before he could seek help or reassurance of the love of his family. He has been gone for over eight years.

We were victims being hounded by terrible death brought on through alcohol, drugs and depression. Only a short time ago, we were a big, happy family growing up in the mining camps with eleven children. By the time this story is done, we will be down to four.

Steve and Sharon came for a visit and we all decided to have a Bible study at our house. Boy, the Lord was doing miracles in our lives! Through my growing process, I quit drinking and began living for the Lord. By now everything in the Bible was starting to make sense. As a family, we drew closer than ever. The kids were happy and content. Coming home from school, they would find me with hot chocolate and cookies or rolls. Sometimes we would have a special treat, Indian fried bread and tea. That year I made them some new mukluks, worked at the clinic and kept my house spic and span. Sonny and his friends went to the Teen Club on Friday nights. Jody Ann was getting old enough to spend the night with her friends.

Packing her clothes and her Cabbage Patch Kids, she was a bit hesitant about her first night away from us.

That night at 10:00 P.M., a car drove up with her, hugging her *Cabbage Patch Kids*, just like I used to do to Sara.

8

Convicted

One year later I was on a bender again and for the last time went to counseling. I heard the same thing over and over. *There is no cure for alcoholism. It is a disease.*

That was their philosophy. The thing they didn't know was that I had Jesus. He forgave me and so did Mike. On April 14, 1986, I asked Jesus to help me overcome my Alcoholism. I prayed so hard that day, there were tears in my eyes. A wino in the bed next to mine was drying out at the Detox center. I wasn't a wino, but I was just as sick as he was. I looked around the room and saw whites and Indians, sleeping and suffering next to each other. The color of our skin made no difference, we all had the same problem. We were helping one another by pouring juice or whatever. Some of us that had been there for a few days would help by serving trays or getting things set up for the new patients coming from a shower.

The Lord was convicting me. If it wasn't alcohol that was going to kill me, it would be guilt!

A few days later, my nine year old daughter, Jody Ann wrote me this letter:

Dear Mom,
I love you very much. We miss you. Come home.
Love,
*   Jody.*
P.S. Mom!
YOUR HEART IS IN US! Mom, I'm sorry for lying. DON'T DRINK!
Mom, please stop. DON'T DRINK AT YOUR BIRTHDAY!

It was then I knew I would be able to never touch alcohol again. The letter had tears coming down from faces she had drawn and bottles that represent beer with X's all over them. Mike and the kids were waiting. We talked and hugged and cried and I could tell for the first time that Mike too was a changed person. I still carry this letter around in my Bible and I am going on my seventh year of sobriety. PRAISE THE LORD!

My part-time job at the clinic and my duties at home kept me busy most of the time. At the clinic, there was one primary Health Aide and two alternates. Whenever the primary wasn't there, one of us would go in and cover for her.

On a day when I was on call, my niece Debbie went into labor. I immediately whisked her onto a mail plane and into the Fairbanks Hospital. During the flight, I was probably worse off than my patient. Once there it was like saying, "Here, she's all yours." Fifteen to twenty minutes later, Michael Eugene was born by Caesarean section. Another time when the primary aide was out of town, my friend, Lynn's baby decided to arrive two weeks early. Again, in the middle of the night, I called the local pilot to fly us in. I believe this pilot could fly his plane with his eyes closed. Lynn is a special, dear friend of mine and a freelance writer for the Northland News. Her husband, Don, is a teacher and they have three children.

My niece Debbie and Michael Eugene.

A job is a job in a small town. You'd take it whether you like it or not, but I just so happened to love mine. I never got bored or ran out of things to do. The two sisters that I worked with were very nice and taught me a lot, which I thank them for. One of the last trips I made into Fairbanks before I moved to Wyoming was with a patient who was a relative. Following doctor's orders over the phone, I ordered medivac for this person who was bleeding to death. As soon as we got to the emergency room, they had to do a blood transfusion. Eventually, the gastritis healed up with time and prayers. And so goes life in my busy little hometown of Eagle, Alaska.

As I look back today, it has been pretty close to six years since Mom died of a perforated ulcer. She was a strong woman considering what she had been through. Once a nurse asked her, "Louise, how do you handle all these tragedies?" She answered by saying, "I pray all the time."

The pain from her ulcer was all over her face as she had us call Isaac from his job with the National Park. Mom knew she was dying and we all knew what to expect. Then she asked to see Silas, her son-in-law. She was tough to the end. Two days later, she was laid to rest next to Dad.

I didn't need alcohol to help me through this time. I had the Lord and for the first time, I wasn't angry at God. I was free to feel blessed at knowing Mom had gone home to the Lord. She had grieved and suffered enough. Right now, she's at a place the Indians refer to as the "Happy Hunting Ground."

At the memorial service, there were grown men and women whom Mom had delivered as the Eagle mid-wife or as the first volunteer community health aide. Like Dad, she served strangers tea and a bite from her cabin. Her best friend, "Goodies Grandma," was there comforting us.

Life at Eagle seemed to promise a leveling out to us. Mike, the kids and I were busy farming potatoes and hay near our cabin above the village. We also tended a big garden. Mike had had three horses for several years. He used them to skid logs, haul firewood, or for transportation to church in the city. It was hard for me during the winters, but I kept going to church, even when temperatures hit 20 to 40 degrees below zero. Then our beat-up old truck which we had bought from Ben would quit on us. We called that truck the "Red Dog." Mike sold pota-

Our hayfield in Eagle.

toes and logged, while I worked at the clinic; we were living a pretty good life and making ends meet. Our freezer was full of salmon, moose, caribou, berries and fresh garden goods. We had been able to get electricity to our house; eventually, we would have a phone and TV. With state grants from the pipeline revenues, the village put in a well with showers and a laundromat. Life was easier and I was really enjoying it.

Sonny was growing up, a good kid, maybe a little spoiled. He still kept company with Steve and Sharon's boys. As he got in his teens, he put a dogteam together and spent a lot of time mushing. I would help cook for his dogs sometimes, recalling the days when he and I had cooked for Mike's dogs at the trapline cabin. He used to say, "Someday I'm going to be a musher!" He had good heros; some of the famous mushers such as Clyde Mayo. Today, Clyde is married to Kathy Stevens, who is another granddaughter of Sophie and Art Stevens'.

Kathy's father was Walter Stevens. Walter left Eagle in his early teens, went to a boarding school, then entered the Navy and finally graduated from the University of Alaska as a civil engineer. He met his wife, Betty while in college and they had four children,

Mike and his sawmill in Eagle.

Jimmy, Kathy, Becky and Brian. Walter was the first native to receive a degree in civil engineering, according to a conversation I had recently with Betty. Walter was only 32 years old when his pickup went through the ice on a pond and he drowned. Betty is proud of the family she raised, all with families of their own now. She has remarried and lives with her husband, Ralph Moore at Walden, Colorado, only forty-five minutes from my Wyoming home.

One winter Sonny went to a mushers' seminar in Fairbanks. His heros were there; George Attla, Susan Butcher, Gareth Wright and his friend Mike who is the B.I.A. superintendent in Fairbanks.

Further into his teen years, Sonny had some rebellious times. Like a typical teen, he was doing things behind our backs. We prayed and learned to trust the Lord and his Word through these times of growing. In Proverbs 22:6 the Word says: *"Train up a child in the way he should go, even when he is old, he will not depart from it."*

And Isaiah 44:3 says: *"I will pour my spirit upon your*

Mel, Ellen and Arthur.

seed and my blessing upon your offspring." During this period, our peace was marred when Sara's husband Junior died, too young, from a heart attack. Facing life alone with three kids after helping bury most of her family was hard for Sara and she, like so many others, sought comfort from alcohol. Alcohol betrayed her and killed her much sooner than any of us could have expected. Her children were scattered; Willard lived with Aunty and Uncle, Corrine was in Tok and David was in a foster home at the North Pole. At the end, she fought for life in a three day battle. She clung to our hands and cried. Her children were all there hoping and praying for more time with her as were the rest of the family. I remember vividly holding my sister's hand at the last and talking to her about the Lord, holding back tears, trying to give her love and strength to live. But, we couldn't keep her with us. The Lord was my strength through these sad days, I didn't need alcohol. The loss of their only surviving parent was so hard on her children: Our sweet Corrine, who looks so much like her mom that our hearts broke to see her; Willard and David, who've always supported one another; they clung together now in confusion and pain. If you had seen my sister's kids that day suffering from the loss and destruction brought on by alcohol, the sight would move you to give up drinking if nothing else would.

Sara was buried next to Junior in the Eagle City Cemetery. Oh, Sara dear, I hope you are at peace. I have thought of you a lot and missed you so much as I wrote of our childhood days in Coal Creek and Woodchopper when you were there every morning when I awoke and were in the center of every one of my days.

Isaac graduated from college with a Bachelor's Degree in Land Management. I went to Fairbanks to attend the ceremony with Sandi and all their kids, Margie, Eddie, Lisa and Christy and Sandi's mother Elsie who came from Arizona to celebrate with her son-in-law. It was the happiest we had been for a long time. Watching Ike finally get his diploma brought tears to my eyes and I thought of how proud Mom and Dad would have been to see him. We had a potlatch, but this time for a *HAPPY* occasion. We had a real proud uncle that day. The next day as I was rushing around to go home to Eagle, I picked up a Fairbanks newspaper because my brother made the front page.

One hot summer day as I was busy canning salmon, a social worker called from Fairbanks and asked if Sara's

Sonny, Conan and James Barr Fraser III on the Yukon River.

son, David, could come home for a visit and stay with us for two weeks. "Of course he can!" was my answer. David was 15, but small for his age.

While he was at our home, Sonny took him fishing on the river alot, using our boat with a 15 hp engine. Jody

Ann and David had some adjustments, getting used to each other. They were at each other like brother and sister, competing for a space as if they thought there wouldn't be room for both. Good old peacemaker Sonny gave me a break many times. He would take one of them on a boat ride or do things with them to help keep them out of my way. One day, I took them to pick berries near our cabin. I think on that day, Ellen and I did most of the berry picking while Jody Ann and David did all of the bickering!

But, the two weeks were up before anyone expected and David had to go back to the foster home. As I

Isaac's College Graduation, L. to R.; Eddie, Margie, Sandi, Isaac, Lisa and Christy, Elsie Leider in front.

watched him get packed and ready to go, his little face was sad and long, saying to me, "I don't want to leave."

Mike and I had some heavy decisions to make and probably some big challenges to overcome now that we had gotten in contact with David. Should we take him or not? Could we have him or not? Would he want to really stay or not? We prayed and talked it over, then we talked with Sonny and Jody Ann who were eager to have David come. We called David and asked him if he would like to live with us. He was overjoyed, outrageously excited and ready to come right away! David was in the custody of the state, so we expected to run into legal problems to have him come and live with us. We began by petitioning the state with the help of the Indian Child Welfare Act from Tanana Chiefs Conference (T.C.C.) an Indian organization in Fairbanks. We were successful in gaining custody of David. We were offered state foster care money, but we refused. Instead, we accepted Junior's Social Security support to help with David's clothes, medical expenses and other needs he might have. The state money was probably twice as much as the money he gets from his father, but all we wanted to do was help David and have him know we cared. Oh, my dearest Sara, maybe here I can help make up for your loss by loving and caring for your son.

My heart went out to David. This kid needed his family and we wanted to have him with us. But, there were concerns which could not be swept under a rug. David was a full-blown FAS child and as a health worker, I knew the down and dirty days we would all face. I kept saying to myself, " *With God all things are possible.*" But how could I know what I was getting myself into! Nothing prepared me for the changes in our life when we added a new kid, well started towards growing up, with different tastes, habits, attitudes from ours! God strengthened us all, the Potts family and David, because it was His will that we should be a family, and He wasn't going to ditch us in the middle of our growing.

Mike was very patient. Sonny and Jody Ann were having fun introducing David to everything as 'family' now, not a guest; dogs, horses, chickens, wild spruce hens, chores, fishing.

It wasn't long before David learned to help Mike or Sonny feed the horses and put them out in a pasture. Riding and harnessing skills came next. David was a special child and because of his health problems and small size, he had been indulged and spoiled rotten. And, of course, Sonny and Jody Ann had their special routines in the family and were attached to their particular place in the 'line-up'. All three kids seemed to have three occupations; school, chores and driving me crazy! So many times I've wondered, "How am I going to make it with three kids? Especially with David being so hyper." To this day, I really don't know, but the Lord does and He hasn't burdened me with His methods, He has just held my hand through good days and bad ones. And there are steadily more good days.

My little nephew is now over 5'4" tall, has been basketball manager for two years and even joined the track team this spring. He can saddle a horse as fast as any cowboy in this state, I do believe! The summer of 1991, he got himself a summer job with the Forest Service and recently he bought a letterman's jacket and plans on buying some school clothes and a gun so he can hunt for elk and deer. David is a responsible young man with a good outlook on life and a big love for the Lord. Someday he will be a welder or an artist or BOTH!

My niece Sophie.

9

Encampment, Wyoming

In the Spring of 1989, Mike and I discussed moving to the lower 48. I was really happy and excited as were David and Jody Ann. Many years had passed since I had left Alaska, and they had been there all their lives; we weren't prepared for the homesick feelings we would have. But, as with any other problem, the Lord helped us, leading us to a church family and Christian friends who would strengthen us and be a mirror of the calling God had for us in ministry.

By the time we were deciding, Sonny had been reunited with his biological father and stayed in Alaska with him for a time. We felt we needed the change to offer better opportunities to the kids and most of all, to be closer to Mike's family.

With three horses and some of our belongings in the back of our stock truck, we headed for Wyoming. We made it to our destination in eleven days. The country was different, but as beautiful in its way as we hold Eagle to be.

That summer, while Mike was logging, we camped in a frame tent until we bought our mobile home in August. Later, in September, Sonny joined us for his senior year. He graduated from Encampment High School on May 19, 1990. This is the kid that we were told had *learning disabilities*. Two days before graduation, he borrowed my first and most precious car and got his driver's license, all by himself. The written test was "a piece of cake," he told me. Sonny is tall as are all the Juneby boys

Sonny's senior picture in Encampment.

and built stout. In June of 1990, he headed back to Alaska and is still living there. We miss him, it is hard to have so many miles between you and one of your kids. But we are near in spirit and love, and we lift him up in prayer continuously. "Cheek Cheek" was the name Mom gave to him when he was a baby.

Jody Ann, now sixteen, is 5'6" tall and slender, with a bright, Miss America-type smile, long, shining, dark brown hair, and big, beautiful, dark brown, 'Indian Princess' eyes. Her Indian name, *Gow Cho*, means "Big Eyes." In her first year of high school in Saratoga, WY, Jody Ann played basketball and made some good friends. She bought a registered quarterhorse mare and loves riding with her friends, Bryony and Amy Vyvey, daughters of Ray and Jennifer Vyvey of Saratoga. They sort of adopted Jody Ann, kind of like the way the indian people did with the kids in my village.

Our life in Wyoming is great. I've grown to like the country, along with the people. It took awhile to get used to the desert look, but this is my home for now until the Lord directs us to another place. I have found the people responsive to and interested in my Native American beadwork and leather art. The people here have to work very hard, long days just as in Alaska and I think this affects the energy people have to expend on prejudice and there hasn't been much of a problem. I have worked at the Valley View Nursing home different times when my schedule allows for it, continuing my health care field. The adventure of moving to Wyoming has stimulated me to make other adventurous trips.

One of the most exciting things I have done and one I will never forget was to take part in The National

Clockwise from left; Conan, Regi, Bill,
Shyanne and Shawna in Phoenix.

Congress of American Indians conference in Albuquerque, New Mexico.

I heard there were going to be people at the conference from Fairbanks, so I headed for Laramie in my Chevy Celebrity station wagon to catch a bus to Albuquerque. I was flabbergasted—the bus station in Laramie was closed. Without a ticket, there was no way I could get on the bus. "Now what do I do?" I thought. I knew the bus was coming toward Laramie from Rawlins and maybe, "I can race and beat it to Cheyenne." I mumbled to myself. Butterflies swarmed through my churning stomach. Driving through the darkness toward Cheyenne on the lonely interstate, I was worried how I would get along in Cheyenne traffic. I had driven *through* the city twice, coming back from Denver the summer before with Mike and the kids. But, this time, I was *alone* and I had to negotiate my way through the city to the bus depot.

No matter how fast I drove, once I got to Cheyenne, I found the bus beat me there! It was just pulling out. There was no chance to buy a ticket. I looked at my watch and decided to go for it to *DENVER*.

I had only gotten my very first driver's license a year before in Wyoming. Going into Denver with five lanes racing south, the people 'drove for blood' and as if they would cheerfully run me over as I tried to get into my lane on the right. The Lord was with me, preventing accidents and I said aloud, "Thank you, Lord," as I took an exit which led me downtown. The skyscrapers reminded me of the Tower of Babel in the Bible. With a sigh of relief, after running through a red light, I finally found the bus depot and was able to get aboard a bus for Albuequerque. Mike's sister, Cindy, and her husband, Dave, came and picked up my car, taking it to their home. Safe and sound on the bus, but exhausted, I thanked the Lord for watching over me.

At the conference, I went up to a lady leaving the conference, the first person I had spoken to, tabbed her on the shoulder and asked, "Excuse me, could you—" She turned and—*It was SANDI, Isaac's wife and my sister-in-law!* What a small world!

Jody Ann, Mike, Me and David at the Foothills Baptist Church.

What a wonderful week with the dried fish the Alaskan natives brought down. Later during that first day, I saw Sarah James coming down the hall. Sarah was an old friend from my hippie days in San Francisco. What a reunion! There were so many friends from Fairbanks I felt like I was home in Alaska, except we were in the Hilton Hotel. Kathy Mayo and I shared a room in the Governor's suite because there were no other rooms available.

After a week, we were pow-wowed out! It was time to say good-bye. I was okay saying farewell to all my friends on Saturday night until the time came for Sandi to leave. To part with her was an emotional, difficult time. Once back at our room, Kathy took me out to a nice dinner, then we watched TV for the rest of the evening and tried to get ourselves wound down. On Sunday I made the trip back to Wyoming and lived to tell about it!

In March, 1991, Jody Ann and I got a chance to go home

In Winter Park Colorado, L to R.; Dave Cyganiak, cousin
Laura Semanche, David, Me, Gramps and Jody Ann.

to Eagle for two weeks. We caught our flights out of Salt
Lake City. As we drove to Ogden to spend the night with
Jo Ellen Worner, a former teacher in Eagle, a car pulled
out in front of us just as we were merging with the traffic.
I praised the Lord for getting us through another close
call.

During our visit, our great Chief Andrew Isaac died
peacefully in his sleep. A year before we moved to Wyoming, Mike and I got a chance to visit with Andrew while
he was in the hospital. There was no doubt about his
faith in the Lord. I can still hear his powerful speech at
the conventions in Fairbanks. He would always start off
with a prayer as his words echoed across the hall, "You
younger generation . . . ."He stressed to hang onto our
Indian way of life and to be proud of our heritage. Now
the great Chief sits up yonder, waiting for his younger
generation. I can only think of how he and Dad must be
rejoicing in *The Happy Hunting Ground*.

In August, 1991, I was led to go to Des Moines Area Community College in West Des Moines, Iowa. We lived with Mike's folks. Mike finished some work in Wyoming, then headed for Iowa to work for a time, before we all returned to Wyoming. I concentrated on my liberal arts courses necessary to achieve a nursing degree. My goal is to complete the courses necessary to go into fulltime nursing. I feel the Lord leading me toward a nursing career which I can use in His service. DMACC reminded me of my high school days in Oregon, except I was one of a few Indians at the college. Everyone I met was so nice and helpful. While there I got involved in the Campus Crusade for Christ group, a nationwide organization of Christians. Before I left, I was interviewed by a reporter for the Des Moines Register who wrote about my book, my intentions and my being a born again Christian very sensitively and well. I have friends in Encampment whose family lived near Des Moines and who saw the article and contacted my friends about it. Copies of this article and another in the Saratoga Sun in Wyoming were sent to Eagle and Fairbanks and helped get the contacts going for publication of my story.

Researching for my psychology class especially and other studying led me to spend a lot of grey, dreary winter days in the West Des Moines library. While there, I ran across a book written my Dr. Ernest Patty called *North Country Challenge*, which contained his experiences in Woodchopper and Coal Creek as well as so much other interesting information. My heart leaped with joy; contact with my home and childhood. I checked the book out and raced home, dodging more big city traffic, to show it to my family. I was amazed that some of the very things Dr. Patty had described were the same things I had written about in my story.

In keeping with the old saying, "It's a small world", across 2,000 miles and 42 years, I met Al Ames' nephew, Dan Hall, right in Encampment, WY. Dan is a big man with a ready smile. My first impression of him was, "He looks more like a football player than a logger."

"He reminds me of Paul Bunyan," commented his

99

wife-to-be, Kim.

A few nights ago, as I was working on this story, the phone rang. Dan and Kim were calling. "My Grandma is here and she would like to meet you all." Dan said. We went right over and sitting in the living room was a nice looking lady with snow-white hair, Hazel Ames Richards, and her daughter Margaret. We hugged like we had known each other for years.

After two years of writing, I am nearly to the present day of my life's story. Many, many pages were written by hand on the pages of wirebound notebooks, until I was able to get a typewriter.

On the following pages, Mike has written his version of our best and last year on the trapline.

Remember, the Lord makes miracles happen when least expected. If you ask the Lord for forgiveness, He is faithful. Likewise, you must forgive others who have done you wrong or hurt you and don't forget to pray for them too.

David graduated on May 23, 1993.

Jesus was on the cross, died for all of the world and whosoever believeth in Him shall not perish but have everlasting life. While on the cross He spoke to His father and cried out to Him. He said, "Father, forgive them for they know not what they do."

God gave his son on the cross for sinners like me. It was all in his plan to save sinners of the world. He loved us so much that He gave His only Son for the sins of the whole world.

I pray that you will be touched and moved by our testimony. I realize that I made a mess out of my life. The devil, trickster that he is, thought he had me, but there is one who is more powerful and in control. That is JESUS CHRIST, THE SON OF GOD. Once I was hell bound, now I'm Heaven bound. What a wonderful feeling, knowing that.

My one piece of advice to the street people in Fairbanks, Anchorage or any other city is that you go back to your village, or reservation: get involved. Your people need you and you need them. We will pray that you, the reader, whether you're in a bar, on a street, in Detox or wherever, will get on your knees and cry out to God.

God is easy to talk to. You can use your own words to accept His love and salvation, or you can use these suggested words:

"Great Spirit Jesus, forgive me of my sins. I believe you are the Son of God, that you died for my sins and that you arose from the grave on the third day to sit at the right hand of the Father. Cleanse me and fill me with the Holy Spirit. Thank you for saving me. Amen."

In Hebrews 13:5, the Word of God says: "*I will never desert you, nor will I forsake you.*"

Remember this promise, believe the Lord can heal, have faith and trust in Him. Make new friends and keep the old ones too. Go to church and study God's Word. May God go with you as you,

WALK BY THE SPIRIT.

Jody Ann won second place
in the Wyoming State History Day competition, and
won a medal at the National History Day Competition
in Washington D.C. for outstanding state entry.

II

10

Our Last and Best Season on the Trapline

• By Mike Potts

Introduction

Since white men came to America, there's always been those who want to go out past the edge of the frontier—the "Mountain Man." Every generation 'till the Lord comes again will have these renegades of civilization. Well, I was one of these renegades that was blessed with fulfilling that desire.

I went to Alaska in 1968, June 5th, 10 A.M., a day after graduation from high school. I was 17 years old. In the 21 years of living in the Alaskan bush I have been fortunate enough to do a variety of occupations. I've worked on commercial fishing boats, worked for Fish and Game, worked as horseback guide and transporter for hunters, worked on the Alaska Pipeline, fought forest fires, as well as run the trapline with dogs for 9 years.

When I moved to where I was to call home in 1971 I lived in an Indian village on the banks of the Yukon River (when not on the trapline)—From this village I married my wife in 1975. We have a son and a daughter, all of whom have traveled the mountains and rivers of our part of Alaska with me the old fashioned way—dogs, on foot, or with horses.

We quit the trapline in 1980, started a sawmill and farmed using horses for power. I logged with horses. I also packed hunters into the mountains with the horses till we decided to do something different. We loaded up the stock truck with gear and horses and belongings and moved to Wyoming to log with the horses and to ride horseback around the mountains and of course hunt elk and fish for trout

But this story is about the best season we had on the trapline. It was also the last one for me. The year—1979, the place—somewhere in the eastern interior of Alaska, (You don't need to know where. Its better you find your own country on your own)—I was 29 (and by now was at the age I was beginning to have a little sense). My wife about the same age, our son 8, and our daughter 2, and along with our 4 sled dogs, we begin this story.

I hope you find it enjoyable and maybe helpful.

This story is dedicated to renegades like me—May God have mercy on your souls and lead you to the Lord Jesus Christ.

Gearing Up For The Trapline

For us the trapping season starts along the banks of the Yukon River, even though our trapline is 50 miles out in the mountains, because our sled dogs have to eat and the cheapest source of dogfood is that which the Lord put in the river—Dog Salmon. There's a large run of these fish that come up the Yukon every fall heading on up to their spawning grounds in the headwaters of the Yukon River in Canada. And so, with a couple of 60 foot gillnets placed in eddies. along the bank of the river you'll catch your supply of dog food. I usually figured 125 salmon per dog, of which I ran a four dog team. So 500 Dog Salmon would do the job.

I'd set the nets the last couple days of August and try to be done fishing by the 13th or 14th of September. The salmon run would start slow, but by the 8th or 10th of September I'd be catching 50 to 80 a day or more. I'd split, hang and semi-dry the salmon we'd caught till the 10th then I'd leave whole the rest I'd catch. It's cool enough by the 10th of September that the flies pretty much stop buzzing around.

A typical day begins at 6:30 A.M. and after coffee and such I'd be in my boat heading to my nets. It would take about two hours to pick both nets and get back home. I'd usually leave the catch in the boat and go have breakfast then go down and cut and hang fish which took another hour or two depending on how good the catch was.

The rest of the day would be spent repairing gear or getting air drops ready. Air drops are our food and necessary items for the trapline. We pack them in burlap bags and wrap them with strapping tape till they are rock hard. Any part that is loose will explode on impact. The air drops are dropped out of a low, slow flying airplane at a prearranged time and spot. This way you don't have to build an air strip, which is good because you'll have enough trouble with bears tearing your place up without having to worry about someone flying in and taking things. The dried and whole salmon are just tied into loose bundles and thrown out of the plane without much trouble. (See appendix for grub list for four months.)

Dog Packing Out To Trapline

We always try to leave on the 16th of September figuring a week to get to the main cabin on the trapline. (Main cabin is where we base out of for trapping.)

Our system is simple. We pack our food, tarp (a piece of plastic), cook gear, and my sleeping bag on our dogs. My wife and son would each carry their sleeping bags and change of clothes on a pack board which wouldn't be more than 15 lbs., and which they could handle and I'd pack our daughter, who was then two years old, on my back.

Day One:

The first day leaving the village I'd have had our nephew drive us out on a gravel road about 17 miles into the mountains to our summer-fall trail. Heading out from there it was only 37 miles to our main trapline cabin, but it's pretty hard going compared to mountains in western USA. The footing is often spongy and rough or brushy, or steep and rocky. Because of the difficulty for my wife and kids, six miles is a good day.

As we'd get to the trail-head, (there's no trail really, its just where we start from), we unload dogs, gear and family. Getting started with dogs is the hard part.

They want to explore everything but somehow we get them packed and started off. This is bear country, Grizzlies in particular, so we've got our rifles ready at all times. Our boy carries our .22 and shoots Ptarmigan as we go for added meat.

The travel would be slow. We'd stop a lot but the day is beautiful, mountains still would have some colors left and one would feel good to be underway with no real time pressures on us. We'd have ten days till the air drops at main cabin are due so there's no rush.

We'd make six mile camp about 3:30 P.M. it's on an open bench above a brushy creek right at timber line so the view is good. There's enough dry wood for a campfire, water not too far away, poles to make frame to put tarp on for a lean-to. It's 4:30 or 5:00 P.M. and mom gets supper going over the fire, the kids are playing, dogs are chained each eating 1/2 dried Dog Salmon, and me, I'm on my back, cup of tea in hand, enjoying the good life. Supper on the trail, before we get meat, is usually macaroni and cheese. It's easy and stays with you and if we get any Ptarmigan we fry them on the side. Other than crawling into sleeping bags in our lean-to the day is done.

Day two:

The day would start out nice and frosty. I would get a fire going and put on coffee pot which had a layer of ice on it. The fire sure felt good. We aren't in a rush to break camp 'cuz the frost on the brush would get our pants wet. I cook breakfast—boil a pot of rice and raisins, put some dried milk, butter, and sugar in it and then get kids and wife up. We would eat and then take our time breaking camp and packing dogs, then we're off. The brush is still a little wet but not bad.

We climb up hill all morning. The first half of the climb would be spongy with poor footing then it would kind of top out before the next leg. As we'd head down to the creek, we'd see clouds coming. By tonight it might snow some. We'd get down to a creek and follow it for several miles till we'd decide to camp. Our daughter was a good little traveler, not complaining, just sitting in her little pack board seat looking around. The dogs did good, too, and didn't run off. We didn't see any game today. We made camp down aways on the creek. Got camp set up, fire going, dogs fed and bedded down, put extra wood under lean-to 'cuz it looked like it could get wet, and built fire close to it. Its raining now but feels like it could turn to snow. May as well eat supper and get into our bags and read a western.

Day three:

Woke up to snow and it's still coming down. We had a good camp so instead of getting wet and getting our daughter cold we'd lay over a day and see if it gets any better. Kept fire going and read westerns, drank a lot of tea, and played with the kids. Maybe it's not a bad day.

Day four:

We woke up to snow on the ground and partly cloudy skies. Best get going so we broke camp, packed dogs and put on the "big skedaddle." We have eight miles to go but my line cabin closest to town (about 35 winter trail mile's from town) is there waiting with wood split and ready for firing up the stove. But we have a long climb and lots of brush to go through until we start the last two miles down to the cabin, and 4 inches of wet snow on top of that-we'd best get started. Everyone, dogs too, seem to be holding up o.k. We stop a lot but as we start the last two miles to cabin, our daughter starts crying. Her feet are cold. I cut my wool jacket under my arms, take off her rubber boots, and stick her feet inside my jacket. This helped but she was still uncomfortable and still cried a little. We saw some caribou but didn't want to shoot any till we'd get to the main cabin.

Finally, we came to the bluff above the creek (I won't say the name of the creek) and see the cabin across it over yonder saying "Come on in." The cabin hadn't been hit by bears this time. We always took everything out of the cabin and put it in the cache, then leave the door open. I'd find when I'd close the door if a bear would come by the pesky varmint would get mad and tear things up. When the door would be left open he didn't do the damage as with door closed.

At last we'd get to the cabin and get a fire going, These little line cabins warm up fast and so does our daughter. The cabin is 9x9, and has a bunk in back full length of back wall, shelves and small table against one side, and stove and wires for drying wet clothes on the other side. There are two small windows, one on each side, split pole roof with sod on it, and a dirt floor. When you would come in cold, wet, tired and hungry enough to eat a wolverine, hide and all, you see the shack like a Hilton Hotel! Anyway, we make it to the town end of the trapline and feel like we're home. By the way, the bunk is made up of poles with wild hay cut and laid on them with canvas tacked over the hay. The bunk is 3 feet off the floor. You'll see why when it's 40 below.

Day five:

We stayed at the cabin this day. I wanted to get in some wood for the season; needed to pull toboggan down off cache for the coming winter season and there were a few odds and ends that needed doing. Always liked this place. It has a rocky mountain in back of the cabin with sheep on it and high ridges that reach well above the timberline. This is caribou country with good winter moose range as well as sheep on ridges.

Day six:

We'd eat another hearty breakfast of rice and raisins, load up, and head out. The snow was gone. We're following our trapline trail down this creek valley. It's a fairly broad valley and the trail is over usually hard ground so

Our line cabin.

the going is good. We're going to stop at a cabin we built. We call it the "Mooselick Cabin" because it sets across the creek from the moose lick. If a guy has patience he can get a moose here and sometimes caribou. You just sit on it and wait. It's a mineral lick and they paw at the dirt and lick it. It's only 6 miles to this cabin so it's a short day which is good 'cuz I wanted to get some wood laid up for this winter and do what ever else was needed.

There are a lot of spruce hens along the way so my boy shot a mess for dinner. My wife cooked up a bannock bread, fried up the birds and made gravy. Got good feed tonight. This cabin is about the same as the last one.

Day seven:

Last day! but a long one for the family—11 miles to main cabin and HOME for the next 3 months. As we got to the mouth of the creek, where it empties into a small river, usually it's good going here but water is bank to bank today so instead of crossing at riffles and walking gravel bars we have to walk the last 2 miles in the brush. Finally, we go up, cross (I'd wear hip boots this time of year 'cuz one is always crossing creeks and rivers) and

I'd carry my son across first, then daughter, then Mom. Dogs wade across, then it would be a short walk to the cabin and we found a bear had been there—it was a mess! It took an hour or two to clean up the mess and get things down from the cache. Got a fire going in the stove and Mom fried up another bannock bread, cooked the spruce hens our son shot and made gravy. A good way to end a day. Stars would be out tonight. Got to start the hunt tomorrow. There was a lot of fresh moose sign along the river. I fell asleep thinking about making meat.

The Fall Season On Trapline

Got up, the Eastern sky was just getting gray, and headed down the river to the mouth of the creek we followed before. There's a beaver pond there which had a lot of moose sign around it. Got down to the beaver pond and found a place to stand with good view of the area and waited, I didn't see any new sign from the day before of them moving around. Sometimes the bulls will come down the first half of September, get the cows and go back up the mountain with them so they're only in the valley a few days. Other years they are around most of the fall. I waited around till 9 A.M. then walked up river and back home hunting as I went.

Got home, the kids and wife were up and had breakfast ready and I brought my appetite so ate and sat over a cup of coffee awhile.

Then my boy and I went down to a place where there's a lot of standing dead trees (the wood lot) and we spent the afternoon cutting cord wood—chopping down, limbing, bucking them in. six foot lengths with Swede Saw' and then stacking the wood till snow comes and we can haul them on the toboggan with the dogs. We went back to the cabin to find some tea and biscuits there. Sure tasted good. Sat around for an hour or so then decided to hunt awhile. Went up the creek the cabin is on. Was about a mile up when I heard something strange to my left on the side of the hill. I stopped for awhile, didn't see anything so started on and suddenly heard a

110

crashing of brush. Looking, I saw two young bull caribou cutting across in front of me about 50 yards off. I threw my gun to my shoulder, aimed, and fired at the bull in the lead. He stopped and so did the other. I aimed at the one in the rear and fired and it fell. I aimed to shoot the other but he was down already. We were "making meat."

I knew we wouldn't have time to get them home tonight so I gutted them, spread-eagled them, took the tongues and kidneys, and headed home. The kids and Mom heard the shots and were looking for me when I came home. When I handed Mom the tongues and kidneys she got a sparkle in her eyes 'cuz she, like all good Indians or mountain men, know, life without meat is just "starvin' times." Now on to the good life—tongue soup and kidney gravy. Next to roasted caribou head, these are top of the list of "fit food."

The next morning after a good breakfast of kidney gravy and fry bread, the dogs, son and I went up the creek, cut up and packed caribou back down to the cabin. A dog can pack two hind legs each or two shoulders and a rump. I packed ribs, neck and such. We got back home by early afternoon. We've enough meat to get us by a month or so. Getting this meat right away will take some of the pressure off. However, we must keep hunting to get a moose or more caribou. Without meat we'd run out of the staples that were to be air dropped. The plane will be coming tomorrow, Lord willing.

We heard the plane engine about 10 A.M. then saw the plane coming over the ridge across the creek so ran back of cabin to an open tussock flat where we had pre-arranged for the plane to drop the supplies. As I got back there the plane vas dropping the first pass. Was three bundles dropped. This was kept up until the plane, a 180 Cessna, was empty of cargo for us. Then we'd go out and gather up our supplies and put them on the cabin edge of the flat then with backboards we'd carry them to the cache a couple hundred yards away. Some things would go directly to the cabin (like dried apples for an apple pie).

We didn't quite get done packing when the last plane

load came In. This was mainly fish for dogs and three 10 lb. bags of dog food to cook with whole fish. Anyway, it took us the rest of the day to pack the air dropped bags off the flat to where they were to go. By then, we were hungry. Mom had supper ready for us and we were ready to clean it up. She had some fried tenderloins and gravy, fried potatoes (from dried potatoes), homemade bread, and an apple pie and of course lots of tea. Layed around and read a western and listened to the battery operated radio till bed time.

The rest of the time was spent getting wood cut, things in shape for the coming trapping season, and hunting for a moose. Also, this year was a blueberry year. The kids and Mom would get gallons of them in a short time and make blueberry jam and syrup for pancakes. Life is good.

As September closed and October came in I wondered if the moose would ever come back down to the valley. I kept hunting though and one day by the beaver pond I smelled a bull moose in rut. I wasn't too excited about shooting a bull in full rut. There's no fat on them and the meat tastes awful. Anyway, take what you can get and be glad of it. So I started around the corner of the beaver pond and what do you know—a barren cow was across the other side of the beaver pond just a-looking at me. Well, there was meat and I best dispatch it so I did. Walked over the beaver dam to the moose, It was partly in the water still, but it was no problem gutting it. That was one fat moose. We'd be able to make lard which we were in need of plus all the meat we needed.

After I spread- eagled the moose so it wouldn't sour, I took one fat-encased kidney (about the size of a football) and went home. Mom and kids were happy enough to dance a jig. I guess I was, too. I guess you can figure out what we ate that night.

Next morning we all went down to the beaver pond to cut up and cache moose meat.

Still haven't seen any fresh bear sign. Maybe we won't have any bear troubles.

Anyway, we cut up the moose and moved pieces into

the trees where we'd put the cache and cut poles to make a ladder. Then took some heavy gauge wire we'd brought along and with wire in hand climbed up ladder leaning on the tree all the way to the top tied and nailed wire to one tree then the other tree. Cache built, we stopped and fried up some meat. After eating and drinking some hot tea and letting out a hearty belch, I tied a piece of lighter wire on the eight pieces of meat, then with a long rope we hoisted a piece at a time by throwing one end of the rope over the wire then we'd all grab that end, pull up the meat then Mom and son would hold it and I'd put the ladder up against the wire weighted down by the meat, climb up and tie the meat to the wire. We'd do this time and again until all meat was hung. The lowest point of the hanging meat is a good 13 feet from the ground and at least 5 feet from both trees. This meat cache turned out to be a good one. It was safe from the bears— we didn't lose any meat. Later, when the river froze, we'd come down with toboggan and dog team and haul it home.

It's the 6th or 7th of October and things are freezing and by the 15th it's below zero. Everything is pretty much froze up. However, this year a freakish thing happened. Warm, winds came from the south and things warmed up. There was a miniature break-up and this warm spell lasted about ten days. It was strange because once winter comes here, it stays, but this year it didn't. During this nice weather the kids played outside all day wearing only a light jacket. We've got most everything ready for the trapping season so we just putter around. Mom tanned a beaver hide and made me a beautiful pair of trail mittens.

The Trapping Season Begins

Around the first of November it cooled off. Some things froze up again.

I've been cutting dry salmon up into 2x4 inch pieces for bait in my traps. I put a light wire through the meat and attach it to the poles on marten sets. Dry fish seems to be the most practical bait to use. It brings them in.

113

The long trap line, back up the creek we walked down coming to the trapline, will have to be the last one set because there's not enough snow to have the dogs pull the toboggan down nor are the creeks froze good enough. There should have been snow aplenty by now and everything frozen up by mid-October, but like I said, this was a freak year.

Anyway, I decided to set the line out that the main cabin is on. It's only eight miles long and I could set it out in a couple of days. Unfortunately, in the country I was trapping in, I couldn't figure how to make loops of my lines. Between the creeks the country was pretty rough. So we always had to double back. I'd set this line first and carry what I needed in a pack board.

Most of the poles and traps were out but the lower end of the line had to be rerouted by way of where we shot the two caribou and then stay on that side of the creek for another mile.

A single bit axe is the trapper's main tool. The trail axe with a 2' handle is what I prefer, kept sharp with a file, you'll need it to cut brush and such out of where you want the trail to go; you'll need it to blaze your trail, and of course to make your different trap sets. (For the sets for the marten, wolverine, lynx, and wolf see the appendix.)

The first line to set out goes up the creek the cabin is on for four miles, then goes up a side creek I named "Martin Creek" for another four miles. What with re-routing the line farther off the creek and making new sets, I only went as far as the mouth of "Martin Creek." It was a long day. Was well past dark before I got home, but as I got close to the cabin I saw the light in the window, could hear the radio playing and see smoke and sparks rising from the stovepipe. It made me feel like the long day was worthwhile, knowing there'd be hot tea waiting. As I got closer the dogs started barking and Son came out. "Hi, Dad, did you get anything?," he called out in an excited voice. Then Mom stuck her head out and said, "You sure had a long day. Tea's on." Daughter's little smiling face looked up at me while she held on to Mom's leg. All I can say is "It's a good life!" And I thank

God. Maybe that Christian radio station we listen to is getting to me?

The next day was even longer. I got to where I stopped yesterday, caught one marten—a big nice dark one—at least a $50 bill. I cached it in a tree by the last set I make and went on up Marten Creek. It's a nice day, just barely can see the sun for a little while to the south before it goes behind a mountain. There's only an inch of snow on the ground but it's only ten degrees above zero and things are froze up good but we need more snow so I can use dogs.

Its very important to blaze trail when going up a brushy ridge or you'll lose your trail and might lose traps. You see, once you make a set on your trapline you always just spring traps at the end of season leaving them hanging to be re-baited and set next year. No sense taking traps in 'cuz on these wild country traplines you are the only one fool enough to wander around out there anyway. So don't need to worry about theft.

So this line is done. Time to head home. It's already dark and I'm hungry; picked up the marten I cached, went on my way, caught another where the caribou kill was. Tomorrow I'll set line down river to moose kill on beaver pond.

Woke up in the morning about 5:30, got the fire going, put coffee pot on and got back into the bag till it warmed and coffee started to perk. We've kerosene railroad lamps for light. It does give enough light but no extra. Six gallons of kerosene seem to last us the three months we're out on the trapline. Anyway, get the first cup down sitting in front of stove. By then it's 6:00 and the radio station we can get is on so I turn it on and start breakfast and give Mom a cup of coffee. The kids are still asleep. Got caribou steaks a-fryin' and hot cakes with blueberry syrup. I'm hungry and I eat aplenty. Kids are still asleep as Mom drinks her second cup. It still won't be light for another half hour so I drink coffee and listen to radio.

It's finally light enough to load up pack with bait and extra traps and with my trail axe in hand head down to the beaver pond. It snowed another inch and it's overcast. Maybe we'll get some more.

There are about eight marten sets I put out along the way to the beaver pond. At the beaver pond around moose kill there's a lot of activity. I put a wolverine set out on the hill and set about eight marten sets around the beaver pond. I think we'll have a few marten shortly.

Now it's only about 11 A.M. so went home and am thinking about going on past the beaver pond, head up the creek we came down and set out that line and get toboggan so I can use the dogs. Need to get things ready. Will pack dogs including their harnesses to pull toboggan down. With only 2 or 3 inches of snow it will be tough coming back. I'll be gone four days setting line out but will only take three days to check each time.

I have the dog packs already loaded up to put on dogs. My pack is ready and it's time to kiss the wife "good-bye" and hug the kids. We leave and make good time. Won't have to step and set traps for the first two and a half miles 'cuz I did that yesterday. As I start up the creek above the beaver pond I see some sign of marten moving around. I've all the sets made from the previous years, mostly pole sets and some ground sets for wolverine. All I need to do is bait sets and set the traps that are already there. As I said earlier, I use pieces of dry Dog Salmon for marten bait, but for wolverine I use a piece of lower leg bone of caribou or moose, wire it tightly and then staple wire to a tree using fencing staples, hang it about one and a half feet off the ground. This set is put right next to the trail. The wolverine comes along the trail stealing from marten sets, sees the bait, goes after it and if he doesn't step in trap right off he will while he fights to pull off the bait and you got yourself a piece of fur that's worth probably five marten.

I cover trap by first chopping out the ground where I put the trap so it will be level with ground, lay a few pieces of dry spruce boughs down, then the trap. To cover the trap, I find a big spruce tree with a couple of big roots coming out from it. There is usually a big bed of dry dead spruce needles. This I shovel into a gunny sack for covering wolverine sets. I pour out enough to cover trap, spread it out with spruce bough and take a twig and pull any out that's wedged under trap-pan that would stop trap from springing. The pan should be no higher or lower than the jaws of the trap.

So, as I go up I set traps and cut out anything that fell in the trail that would be in the way of toboggan when I bring it down from the upper cabin. Things went according to plans and I got to Mooselick cabin which is an eleven mile day. It wasn't quite dark. After getting fire going and tea water on, I sawed up some more wood. I'd be using this cabin at least seven times before we leave the trapline so will need wood enough so I won't have to cut wood each night. As the winter progresses it will get down to less than six hours of daylight.

It feels about zero temperature outside and is partly cloudy. By the time I drink a cup of tea and saw up some wood it's getting dark out. It's dark inside the cabin so I light a plumber's candle. One of these burns slow enough to last as long as I need it before I go to sleep and till I leave in the morning. I always cache a dozen in each cabin.

Each cabin is outfitted with a frying pan, cooking pot, plates, cups and forks and spoons and such. Also, I leave a bedroll In each cabin so I won't have to carry much and after I get the toboggan running I freight enough grub to each cabin so I won't have to haul grub each time. I even haul some dry fish. This way the less the dogs have to pull, the more you can ride and the less you'll get tired. My personal feed bag is: fry meat, fry bread, and gravy for supper, and for breakfast: fry meat, and boil up a pot of rice, drain it, pour rice in frying pan of meat, stir it up and eat it all. Now, that's "puttin' on the feed bag!"

The next day it's only six miles to the upper cabin and I continue up, setting traps and tidying the trail. There's always more new trees on the trail here than farther down the creek because of wind so it took some time, but we finish the line.

Dogs behaved well, didn't fight or run off and lose their packs.

The cabin's in good shape. Toboggan 's o.k. Looks like

we've plenty of wood. I brought the dog harnesses along so get them strung out and ready for tomorrow.

The next day I had a few wolverine traps to set out on a ridge so went up the ridge, got them out on a ridge that goes up above timberline. So I chopped a small tree down and carried it up the ridge and set the last trap above timberline and wired the trap to the tree I carried up. I dug a small hole in the snow and into the moss and shoved the bait into the hole, laid a little brush on the hole and then covered the trap lightly with moose hair and a little snow to weigh the hair down.

It's definitely below zero today 'cuz the icicles on my mustache are substantial.

It's still early so get back to cabin and hook up dogs and head out and to home. It's a rough ride and a lot of the time I'm running to keep the toboggan from tipping over. There's a marten in a trap before we get to Mooselick cabin. It doesn't seem too late in the day so we press on. Half way to the beaver pond there's another marten. It's already dead and half frozen—a large, good-colored male. By the time we're at the beaver pond it's getting toward dark but at the kill there's two more marten—one in a pole set, the other in the wolverine set and he's a little hard to get out of the trap. They curl up, but I got it out, reset the trap and headed home.

The kids and Mom are happy to see me and I them. Mom has an ability to keep busy and take charge while I'm gone and kids are very creative and can invent things to do and, also, son has school work to do. So they have as much to tell me as I them. We're a pretty good team for this kind of life. Mom also has two apple pies made—one for her and the kids and one for me. I finish the last piece of pie for a midnight snack when I get up to put more wood in the fire.

The next day I hauled wood with the toboggan. At least I don't have to haul it in on my shoulders a log at a time. Hauled the wood from my wood yard we cut this fall. Did this all morning and have a couple of weeks worth. Then in the afternoon I skin marten and watch daughter while son and Mom go set out the little trapline. It's a good life.

118

It's snowing outside. They come back all excited with high hopes of catching marten and rabbits (Snowshoe Hares).

There's more snow out now and today I'll set out the last line. Its only five miles long. That will give me thirty miles of line. So after breakfast I start out. I'll run the dogs straight back behind the cabin and across a flat then onto the river going on up river for a couple of miles. Had a few traps to set on the way then at the mouth of a creek I tied up the dogs and put on my packboard and started up the ridge. It's two miles to timberline and fairly steep. As I go up setting traps, I blaze the trail a little better. I get to top and, Man, it's a pretty view. The trapline is all set out. Now, we'll see what we catch this season.

Now we get into a weekly routine. Monday I'd go up the long line, stay over night at Mooselick, then next day go to upper cabin, chain up dogs, put on snow shoes and go up the ridge to check wolverine sets. Wednesday, go back home, get home by 2 P.M. The next day check the eight mile line then be around cabin and family skinning and stretching fur I caught that week and hauling and cutting wood. I'd be able to run more miles of traps if I could make loops but the country doesn't seem to permit that to happen where my trapline was.

The month of November seems to be the best month to catch marten. I probably caught two-thirds of the catch that month and then it slows down as December goes along.

Wolverine for their size are very strong. When in a trap, they will tear up the area as well as the trap. I've seen them bend trap pans and triggers in such a way it was hard for me to straighten them out.

On the second run up the long line, in the last trap on the ridge above timberline, I caught a very large, very blond diamond wolverine. Somehow caught him on the hind foot. He was mad and it was quite a dance to hit him on the head with the flat end of the axe. But it got done and I didn't get bit. We caught three wolverine that season. Two were large, the blond and a dark one. I sold them for $275 each and caught a smaller female on moose kill and sold her for $250. I did lose about six marten to wolverine that would have brought me $300 but those three wolverine brought $800 so they more than compensated for the theft. I also had three marten damaged by mice pulling hair out of the marten. But Mom made a nice marten hat for Son out of the three so they were used anyway.

Another run on the eight mile line I jumped a grizzly. I was on the ridge u p a creek. I was beside some brush and I heard something break on the other side of the brush. I looked and saw a large grizzly moving around. Then it took off at a run on up the ridge the way I was going. There was a lot of daylight showing under his legs meaning he was an old bear that didn't get enough fat put on to go into good hibernation. I was a little nervous to go on but did and saw that he crossed my trail and kept going. That was the only bear I saw in winter in all the years on the trapline They are mostly fast asleep all winter.

In November we did pretty well. I'd catch about ten marten a week and in December it slowed down till the last week before Christmas we only got four marten. For the two months trapping we ended up with fifty marten and three wolverines. This is just an average season but it made a good wage for us. The traps were already paid for years ago... We couldn't charge the food to trapping expense 'cuz it would cost us more probably if we stayed home instead of trapping. The only real cost we have is chartering a plane for three flights—two for air drops and then the third I have a plane come in and land on the river and pick up Mom and kids and fur. I mush into town with dogs and close down the trapline on my way in and bring in any fur I might catch. Anyway, the plane fare is the only real expense we have. That's only around $300.

The fur auction house I send my fur to (Seattle Fur Exchange) takes a 5% commission out for selling and cleaning fur (I think it's more now) so I end up selling forty-one marten and three wolverine. The marten sold for $2,255 and the wolverine $800 = $3,055 less 5% commission of $152.75, less $300.00 plane bill leaves $2,602.25 which is a fair wage back then.

Some particular traplines on certain years do better. I've heard of one trapper getting over 200 marten in less than 20 miles of trapline, but that's not all that common. The main reason I trapped only till Christmas was I figured any caught later is hurting your breeding stock for next season. Whether I'm right I do not know but that's my reasoning.

About the 17th of December it got pretty cold about 60 below zero and we were wondering if the plane would come in on the 19th. Well it didn't and I'd sprung the two shorter lines the 17th and 18th so we were waiting for the weather to get warm enough for a plane to fly out here to pick up Mom, kids and fur. On the radio station there's a program every night at 9:30 and then at 6:30 A.M. called "Trapline Chatter." If someone wants to get a message to someone on the trapline they call the radio station, tell the message and they broadcast it on "Trapline Chatter." Well the pilot sent a message in and said he'd try to get in to us on the 23rd.

The morning of the 23rd it was a light overcast. It warmed up to minus 40, he might make it in. If he does it will be a marathon mush for me and the dogs into town.

About 9:30 A.M. we heard the plane. We had the dogs hitched to the toboggan ready to go, so we threw our daughter in the toboggan and I headed over to the river where I had marked out the air strip. The plane just landed as we got there. While we waited for Mom and son (they had to walk) we loaded the plane with the fur and personal things. Mom and son arrived soon, boarded the plane and the pilot started the engine, everyone waved and the plane started off. It got off on the first try.

It was just me and the dogs now. The fire in the stove when we got back to the cabin was out so I set the stove out under the overhang, took the things I didn't want to leave in cabin to the cache, then tied the door open so the grizzlies wouldn't tear it down. With that done it was time to leave and if I want to get into town before Christmas morning I'd best put on the "big skedaddle." So we left. As we went along I'd spring the traps. It was well into dark before we got to the Mooselick cabin. Got a fire going, put on snow to melt (after creeks freeze we melt snow for water), then chained up and fed dogs, ate dinner and went to bed.

Next day was Christmas Eve day. We've 91 miles to go today. It's still dark when we leave. It stays that way for the first hour. It's cold too. I've two inches of icicles on my beard already. There's a marten in one trap, then another in next and that's it for marten this season. Get up to upper cabin and I give the dogs a break and I take things I don't want torn up out of cabin and put in cache. The next four miles is up hill and I'll be on snowshoes till we're a mile over the pass. Five miles, then it's down hill till we come to a creek. There we should run onto another trapper's trail. We do, and the trail's broke out but it's been snowed on and drifted in ,too, in spots. Dogs have a slow go. I'm kicking off and running some. We pass a cabin I sometimes stop at. We've another hour and it will be dark. I'm sweating and it must be ten miles to the first cabin out of town. Then its another ten after that so it's going to be all night to get in for Christmas day.

Now we're two hours out of first cabin from town. It's been dark awhile. The dogs and I are getting tired but we've done these marathons before and we've been tired before so we knew what we were getting into.

We finally came to the cabin ten miles out of town. We pulled in. I left the dogs in harness and threw them each a dry fish then went in and built a fire, put snow on and put some frozen chunks of lard and frozen chunks of moose in frying pan. Drink tea and more tea and still more tea and by then the meat was done. Threw a handful of flour in, stirred it in, then poured water on it and stirred that in. Then threw' a couple of frozen biscuits in with the meat and gravy to thaw out a little and ate the whole thing.

I made one near-fatal mistake. I laid down on the bunk—I fell asleep—I don't know how long I slept but when I awoke it was cold in the cabin. Well I jumped up and got my parka on and threw what I had taken out of toboggan back in, untangled dogs and put on the "big skedaddle" again. Times a-wasting and Christmas was here. I guessed it to be 1:00 or 2:00 A.M.

We hit the trail. Dogs knew where we were. The trail here is good. Somebody must have come out here for something from town. Anyway, trail was good. Then we hit the mining road (cat trail) where they use snow machines and trail was great. So another one and a half hours and we were in town. We live four miles the other side of town so pressed on pullin' in front of our log home, banged on the door, and yelled for Mom to wake up. She came to the door and I had made it! It was 5:00 A.M. Christmas morning. I didn't know the Lord Jesus Christ then but I thanked Him anyway for getting us all in safely.

After tending to dogs, I went into the cabin and Mom had a pound of link sausage, 3 eggs, a mountain of hash browns and toast ready. It had been awhile since I had any white man grub. It tasted mighty good. The kids would be waking soon to open presents Mom had bought yesterday. Its a good Christmas. And it was a good season to finish our life on the trapline.

We made enough to buy $700 worth of groceries, a two ton truck for $500, and an old saw mill (not assembled) for $400, and a horse for sliding logs for $900. I'd already paid the pilot before we went, out on trapline that season. So we quit the trapline and began a logging and rough lumber business.

So ends an era in this family's life and we begin another.

I would like to take one more moment of your time to mention something of my spiritual status. I, at this time, was a Hell-bound renegade doing exactly what I wanted, living for myself—not even paying a mind to laws, cursing God, drinking and such foolishness. Then this last season God started dealing with me and through the radio station KJNP North Pole, Alaska, "The Gospel Channel of the North" (and most of the time the only one anyone can get). He convinced me that I was going to Hell and also *"No man by his own works is right with God."* Rom. 3:23. Then He left me in that state for almost two years. Then God sent a man to me to tell the Gospel to me that would save me from going to Hell and spending eternity there. The first thing I had to understand was that *"the wages of sin is death."* Rom 6:23. *"But the gift of God is eternal life through our Lord Jesus Christ."* Rom. 6:23. But what did He do for us that men who trust Him won't go to Hell? This is what had to be explained to me, and was, that He took our sins upon himself and died in our place and was the right payment for our sins because He was without sin. No other man could do this because *"all men have sinned."* Rom. 3:23. Then God raised Him from the grave proving *"Jesus is God."* I Cor. 15:3-4, Rom. 10:9. So I found that *"salvation is by faith not by works."* Eph. 2:8-9.

Life hasn't been easy now that we trust in Christ but we do have peace with God knowing that we are saved from Hell's eternal pain and suffering. We've a purpose now to serve Christ not Satan and sin. I praise the Lord for saving my soul.

End.

Appendix:

Supplies and Trap sets.

The grub list we had for the last trapping season:
1. 200 lbs.. flour
2. 60 lbs. sugar
3. 50 lbs. rice
4. 10 lbs. dried sliced potatoes
5. 25 lbs. pinto beans (less meat means more beans needed)
6. 10 lbs. salt
7. 1 #10 can of dried vegetables (for soup)
8. 25 lbs. dried apples
9. 10 lbs. prunes
10. 50 lbs. lard or shortening
11. 3 lb can yeast
12. 5 cans baking powder
13. 25 lbs. Krustez Pancake Mix
14. 25 lbs. rolled oats
15. 25 lbs. powdered milk
16. Spices: Pepper, cinnamon, seasoned salt, etc.
17. Case toilet paper and one half case paper towels
18. 10 boxes strike anywhere matches
19. 6 gal. kerosene and 50 plumber's candles
20. 5 boxes tea, 3-3 lb cans coffee
21. 2 cans cocoa mix
22. 4 boxes pectin (for blueberry jam)
23. Dental floss for sewing tuff stuff
24. 10 Glovers needles for sewing leather
25. 1 large bottle Betadine (cleaning and soaking wounds)
26. Penicillin Pills
27. 1 tube good topical ointment
28. Tape and bandages
29. Batteries for flashlight and radio
30. Radio booster and antenna wire and radio
31. Nails assorted siizes, staples
32. 3 mill file
33. Swede saw, 3 extra blades
34. Axes and extra handle
35. Hammer, pliers, screwdrivers, crescent wrench, brace and bits
36. 2 rolls mechanic's wire

There are a few other things you might need but this will start you out and with some common sense you can add to list.

What You Should Wear For Winter Travel:

Wool sox, cotton long underwear, heavy wool long underwear, then blue jeans or heavy canvas pants—either will buck wind o.k. or moose hide pants, wool shirt, a couple wool jackets then canvas or moose hide parka with a good ruff to keep wind off face, a qood stocking cap, moccasins or mukluks for colder weather and snowshoeing and shoepacks for warmer days and getting through wet spots. My wife makes winter parkas, pants and moccasins out of Indian tanned moose hide. I've a pair of moose hide pants, made by my wife's mother and a friend, that I've worn since 1973 and they're still in good shape. Moose hide clothes are expensive but last forever. She also makes trail mittens. You'll wear gloves to work in but you'll be wearing mittens most of the time—heavy trail type mitts and lighter mitts. Have plenty of mitten liners and extra felt liners and insoles for moccasins. Frostbite can kill you. Always carry matches in a water-proof case with birch bark or a candle to start fires with—never be without.

Trap Sets:

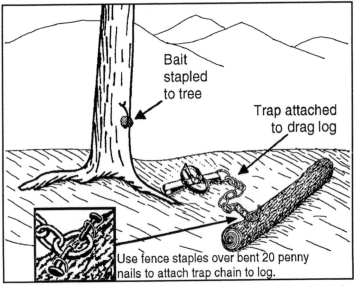

Bait stapled to tree

Trap attached to drag log

Use fence staples over bent 20 penny nails to attach trap chain to log.

Log drag is 5ft. x 3 or 4 ins. Don't use dead tree. Make set right by trapline trail. Rub some beaver castor on tree if you have some.

126

Rub on castor, 16 " up.

Trap with chain looped around 3 ft. tree stump.

Lynx set;
Back in the early 1970's this is the set that I used for Lynx. Lynx are light footed critters so you can't put much, if any, snow on the set. Use a single piece of two-ply toilet paper to cover the trap.
Find a small tree by the trapline trail, cut it off about three feet above the ground. Make a loop in the trap chain and drop it over the stump to the ground.
The Lynx will walk on trail, smell castor (it is a sex stimulant to them), and want to rub against it. Doing so, it will step in the trap. You can also hang a rabbit hide on a string to attract Lynx, tie it about head high to a tree near set.

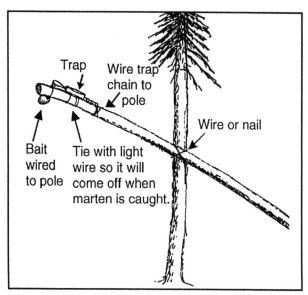

Trap

Wire trap chain to pole

Wire or nail

Bait wired to pole

Tie with light wire so it will come off when marten is caught.

Marten set; Cut down tree to make a post set. Pole should be ten feet, or so, long and three inches in diameter.

127